Praise for Jean-Louis Rodrigue, Scott Weintraub, and *Back to the Body*

"Jean-Louis Rodrigue always brings a personal and positive approach to his coaching work. His involvement is timeless and complete. He is generous, genuine, and creative, [and believes] that even when a character or a story is frightening, it becomes about exploring the work and being of service. Now Jean-Louis and Scott Weintraub have written *Back to the Body*, a book about how to embody the character, giving an enhanced awareness of the purpose and structure of the whole movie, which engages the entire actor's intention and responsibility with the project. Their work is a useful and exciting way to open my channels for my research as an actress."

–Juliette Binoche
Academy Award–Winning Actress

"Now THIS is an amazingly comprehensive roadmap to creating a character. Scott Weintraub is a great actor, teacher, and author. Read this book and become a better actor!!!"

–Jack Black
Actor and Musician

"[Jean-Louis Rodrigue's] technique is inspiring, liberating, and transformational. More importantly, he is a true artist. Being in his presence, reading his words, and engaging in his technique reminded me that regardless of what role I am working on, I can engage with the artist in myself and seek the profound in all things."

–Matt Bomer
Actor and Producer

"Over the years, I've enjoyed working with Jean-Louis to apply the Alexander Technique to performance in new media. His approach to awareness of the body extends beautifully into contemporary technologies like motion capture and volumetric filmmaking. This book is a great reference for preparing to embody characters within production environments that capture the performance of the actor's entire body."

–Jeff Burke
Associate Dean, Research & Technology
UCLA School of Theater, Film & Television

"Having observed Scott Weintraub teach, direct, and inspire students for over 30 years, I am delighted to endorse his wonderful book, *Back to the Body: Infusing Physical Life into Characters in Theatre and Film*, co-written with his colleague Jean-Louis Rodrigue. Scott's performances with our students at Crossroads School (Santa Monica) are now the things legends are made of. Whether it be high drama, slapstick comedy, Broadway musicals, whatever—Scott was able to take students to places they had never been before and all the while to draw from them talents and self-discoveries that make education, and in particular the theatre, so exciting and memorable. To his thorough knowledge of all the elements of drama, Scott brought—as I observed him in action—an improvisational, wild imagination mixed with his genuine zaniness. For students his lessons, scenes, readings, script analyses, and performances were all pure magic. What I didn't fully recognize was Scott's underlying understanding of the role the actor's body plays in developing his or her character. Now we who love the theatre have this exciting book to illuminate that role. *Back to the Body* is a treasure and should become a classic for teachers, actors, directors, curricula specialists—in short, anyone interested in the theatre. It is filled with provocative questions, suggestions, and exercises, all in the context of a philosophy of theatre so complete, we hardly notice what a journey we have been on. Bravo Jean-Louis and Scott!"

–Paul F. Cummins
Head of School
Crossroads School

"I love animal work and what the Alexander Technique has brought into my life. The work allows me to base my characters not just on people and experiences I've had, it opens my world up. What Jean-Louis teaches is invaluable, and I'm so excited he's able to share his wisdom and expertise with so many more artists through this book."

–Zoey Deutch
Actress

"This isn't a book just for actors; this is a gift to the full spectrum of art-makers—artists, administrators, audiences, teachers, and students. What Jean-Louis and Scott illustrate so brilliantly in these pages is how to become completely self-aware and centered in your craft, regardless of your discipline. For a theater producer and teacher like me, their lessons are an indispensable guide to comporting yourself confidently with creative teams; creating environments in auditions, rehearsals, and classrooms that encourage artists to bring their full selves; and leading successful collaborations through artistic generosity, spatial and physical awareness, and a little breath. Learning the principles of the Alexander Technique through Jean-Louis and Scott's contemporary lens, and applying them to your own artmaking, can be life-changing!"

–Andy Chan Donald
Associate Artistic Director,
American Conservatory Theater (A.C.T.)

"Scott and Jean-Louis are both wonderful teachers. Any artist who reads this book will benefit enormously from the creative, eye-opening, and detailed techniques they lay out so clearly. There is a wealth of tips and wisdom in here for any actor."

–Alden Ehrenreich
Actor

"The lessons laid out in *Back to the Body* should be of prime interest to anyone in the performing arts. Inhabiting a character through the body is the way to tap the soul—the mysterious and essential means to unlocking a great performance. Here, for the small cost of a book, are the keys to the city."

–Ron Fassler
Actor and Author

"Frequently, Jean-Louis and I coach in tandem on projects. The actor may take a dream image from my studio to his, and there come to physically inhabit something yet hidden from the rest of us. Or, the actor may arrive at my studio, fresh from work with Jean-Louis, with a wildly alive animal activated in the body that we then add to the mix. I value this collaboration immensely. When I hear that, once again, we are both working with the actor on a piece, I feel a sigh of relief and the excitement of wondering what he has caught sight of. I know that the actor will come from his work awake, breathing, curious, and physically free. We are so very fortunate that Jean-Louis and Scott have translated the depth of their knowledge into *Back to the Body*. I will keep my copy near to me and read it often for the inspiration I have come to rely upon."

–Kim Gillingham
Actress and Acting Coach

"As a writer, I have had the pleasure of witnessing the magic of an actor taking the written word and turning it into action. We strive to turn problems of spirit into problems of technique. *Back to the Body*, by Scott Weintraub and Jean-Louis Rodrigue, gave me insight as to how it's done for the actor, and for that I am very grateful."

–David Milch
Writer and Producer

"The most subtle movements can characterize human behavior in a way even words can't convey. Jean-Louis Rodrigue was instrumental in helping me bring to life three distinctly different 'Waymonds' in *Everything Everywhere All At Once*. Back to the Body will serve as an excellent resource for all actors."

–Ke Huy Quan
Academy Award Nominee for Best Supporting Actor

"I've been an unofficial student and obsessive fan of Scott Weintraub for many years. Both my sons attended Crossroads School in Santa Monica, CA, where Scott taught theatre and acting. At Crossroads, Scott directed several unforgettable productions as part of a school program that has launched the careers of many world-class actors. Observing Scott, what instantly got my attention was the way he coached, inspired, and evoked incredible performances out of so many very young and inexperienced student actors. His productions of Shakespearean plays performed by fifth graders were moving, heartbreaking, and sometimes very funny, and his high-school production of *Candide* was one of the most moving and spectacular in-theatre experiences I've ever had—including shows I've seen on Broadway and in London. I've even hung out before and after Scott's shows with a video camera to see if I could capture how he worked with his young actors so I could steal some of his magic! Well, now it's all here, in this fantastic book. *Back to the Body* contains excellent advice on character research and invaluable suggestions for going deep and specific through physicality—finding the walk, identifying the gestures, and making other fundamental choices about how a character moves. I've worked with many outstanding actors who start by making these same kinds of choices, but I've never seen the process laid out so clearly, so helpfully, and so entertainingly as Scott and Jean-Louis have done in this indispensable book. Potent secrets finally revealed!"

–Jay Roach
Writer, Producer, and Director

"Jean-Louis Rodrigue's method is now an invaluable staple in my preparation for roles. Not only do I have a better understanding of the character, but I also have a better understanding of myself as a whole person, and I can begin to live and breathe the character. *Back to the Body* by Jean-Louis and Scott Weintraub includes all of this training, and I have no doubt that it will prove to be an indispensable resource for all readers."

–Margot Robbie
Academy Award–Nominated Actress

"Jean-Louis came into my life and enlightened me to a new approach in building a character. Through our practice, I've gained a deeper understanding of my instrument. He has helped me expand and integrate my physical life and empowers me to free myself up. Jean-Louis and Scott have been a gift to so many of us and I'm thrilled the world at large will benefit from the wisdom shared within the pages of *Back to the Body*."

–Jurnee Smollett
Actress

"Jean-Louis has been foundational to my work since the early '90s and continues to inform both my acting and directing. When I returned to acting with *Bill & Ted 3*, JL was my first port of call. As anyone familiar with the Alexander Technique knows; the work begins with the body and ends with the body. Jean-Louis and Scott are sorcerers, and this book contains their magic, woven into a highly informative, instructive, and actionable text. Overdue and indispensable."

–Alex Winter
Actor and Filmmaker

"*Back to the Body* captures the energy, precision, and imagination of the actor's training. With personal interviews and examples from his work coaching the stars of stage and screen, readers can delve into the intricacies of Jean-Louis's training and artistic process. He translates the Alexander Technique directly into the language of the actor and offers engaging procedures and relevant exercises to guide transformation. Throughout the chapters, Jean-Louis and Scott continue to bring the focus back to the body, breath, and kinesthetic expression. Their perspective brings to life explorations of the actor's use of body, space, environment, costumes, props, and, most importantly, imagination. Every actor, artist, and person with an interest in creativity should own a copy of this exciting new book."

–Jessica Wolf
Professor in the Practice of Acting at
David Geffen School of Drama at Yale

"It's hard to learn any craft from books alone, but one can gain knowledge from and be inspired by some of them. For acting, this is one of those books. As a writer who relies on actors, entrusting them with my work, I'm glad it was written."

–Steven Zaillian
Academy Award–Winning Screenwriter,
Director, and Producer

"Do we really need another book on acting?" was my thought bubble upon hearing that Scott Weintraub and Jean-Louis Rodrigue had begun writing *Back to the Body*. Having now read the empowering results of their dynamic collaboration, the answer's a resounding, "YES." We have been gifted with a uniquely inspiring, concise, clear, and practical guide to this complex art form. Challenging concepts are made exceptionally accessible in these well-sequenced, organized chapters. I've watched Scott's (beautifully) antic, uber-skilled approach to teaching and directing for some years and marvel at how his giddy liveliness and high-level craftsmanship jump off these pages. This book is a "shiny penny" (as Scott often says of his students) for its directness of language and enticing, exhilarating invitation into the soulful, expansive process of storytelling through performance."

–Zoey Zimmerman, M.F.A.
Theater Director/Educator

BACK TO THE BODY

INFUSING PHYSICAL LIFE INTO CHARACTERS IN THEATRE AND FILM

JEAN-LOUIS RODRIGUE
SCOTT WEINTRAUB

alexander
techworks

Back to the Body
Infusing Physical Life Into Characters in Theatre and Film
Published by Alexander Techworks

Print ISBN-13: 979-8-218-05895-1
E-Book ISBN-13: 979-8-218-05896-8

Copy Editor:	Kate Shoup	Cover Designer:	Nancy Weintraub
Production Editor:	Kate Shoup		Michael Weintraub
Illustrator:	Nicola Maier-Reimer	Cover Execution:	Laurie Dworsky
Photographer:	Todd Domenic Cribari	Models:	Elliyah Banks
Interior Designer:	Shawn Morningstar		Grace Kendall
Interior Layout:	Shawn Morningstar		Tip Scarry
Indexer:	Kelly Talbot Editing Services		Uttera Singh
			Georgina Tolentino
			Lucy Urbano
Proofreader:	CDL Editing LLC		Carson Wolff

*We dedicate this book to all the students, actors, and
theatre and film professionals we have ever worked with,
whose artistry and passion have informed
and inspired our work over the years.*

ACKNOWLEDGMENTS

Our deepest gratitude to our editor, Kate Shoup, for her magnificent skill in editing, organizing, and moving this project forward. Special thanks to our researcher, Internet expert, and scribe, Jill Renner, for her hard work and passion over the years. Thanks also to Michael Weintraub and John A. Farmer for their assistance and input, and to Kelly and Matt Shane for their creative and marketing expertise.

Thank you to all the people who have contributed to this book, allowing us to share their stories and experiences: Gavin Robins, Scott Speedman, Jeremy Narby, Jessica Wolf, Kristof Konrad, Mary McDonnell, Francesca Jaynes, Jeff Burke, Andy Donald, Bo Eason, Dawn Eason, Todd Domenic Cribari, Leonardo DiCaprio, Miguel Esteban, Ilona Katzew, Lynn Hamrick, Pamela Gien, Jack Black, and Kodi Smit-McPhee.

Finally, and most importantly, thanks to our spouses, Nancy Weintraub and Kristof Konrad, whose love, encouragement, patience, and support made it possible for us to create this book.

JEAN-LOUIS RODRIGUE

I am grateful to my colleagues for their support: Lucy Gonda, Catherine Wyler, Maria Furtwängler, Dieter Kosslick, Matthijs Wouter Knowl, Christine Trostrum, Florian Weghorn, Corinne Orlowski, Jana Daedelow, Anja Joos, Kelly McEvenue, Penny McDonald, Natalija Nogulich, Judith Natalucci, Beth Hogan, Beatrice Manley-Blau, Mel Shapiro, Michael Hackett, Tom Orth, Meg Wilbur, Dan Ionazzi, Rich Rose, Jeremy Mann, Edit Villarreal, Bob Rosen, Jose Luis Valenzuela, Joe Olivieri, Brian Kite, Hanay Geiogamah, Nicholas Gunn, Dan Belzer, Perry Daniel, Ed Monaghan, Neal Stulberg, Judy Moreland, Travis J. Cross, Christoph Bull, Peter Kazaras, Ronnie Rubin, and Judy Mitoma.

I want to recognize and thank my mentors and teachers: Herbert Berghof, Sonia Moore, Carlo Mazzone-Clementi, William Ball, Frank Ottiwell, Joy Carlin, Ann Lawder, Allen Fletcher, Bonita Bradley, Frank Ottiwell, Giora Pinkas, Patrick McDonald, Walter Carrington, Dilys Carrington, Marjorie Barstow, Pamela Blanc, Jessica Wolf, Lyn Charlsen Klein, Michael Frederick, Frances Marsden, Judith Stransky, Babette Markus, Judy Stern, Belinda Mello, Penny McDonald, Remy Charlip, Joan Schirle, Misako Tsuchiya, and Bridget Belgrave.

With love and eternal gratitude to Larry Moss, both for the gift of his insightful foreword and for his friendship and profound inspiration for the past 25 years. Thank you to Catie LeOrisa for her generosity and constant support. Thank you to my inspiring theatre colleagues: Sharon Chatten, Nancy Banks, Kim Gillingham, Michael Woolson, Ellen Geer, Natalija Nogulich, Beth Hogan, and Leo Garcia.

SCOTT WEINTRAUB

A very special thank you to my mentors, teachers, collaborators, and directors over the years. From Santa Barbara: Marjorie Luke, Jack Nakano, David Ossman, Frank Condon, and Bradford Dillman. From The Pacific Conservatory of the Performing Arts: Michael Winters, Donovan Marley, and William Frankfather. From Theatre by the Sea: Russell Treyz and Jon Kimbell. From Crossroads School of Arts and Sciences: Paul Cummins, Joanie Martin, and Zoey Zimmerman. Thanks also to my lifelong friend and muse, Virginia Russell.

TABLE OF CONTENTS

Part III
APPROACHING THE SCRIPT THROUGH THE CHARACTER 97

FOREWORD

Having had the pleasure of working with the extraordinary Jean-Louis Rodrigue, first as his student and then having him work with actors and actresses I have directed and coached, I know first-hand the joy of an endlessly curious teacher passionately supporting a student to grow.

Jean-Louis and I worked together on the play *The Syringa Tree*, written by and starring Pamela Gien, who played 23 characters—a daunting task indeed.

The beautiful Alexander Technique work helped Pam transition from character to character so seamlessly, you would have sworn there were men, women, young children, different races, and South Africa in front of you. The narrator was Elizabeth Grace, a 6-year-old white English South African child. At the beginning of the play, Elizabeth played on a swing and danced while she talked to the audience about her life in apartheid South Africa. She then began running and singing, a playful joyous child with the fastest two legs in the universe.

In one step as she reached out her tiny arm, the arm slowed down and those two legs became heavier and more muscular, and Elizabeth's celebration of play turned in one instant into the hard day's work of Salamina Mashlope, a black 39-year-old Xosa nanny, scolding the child for waking her mother, who had a bad headache. That moment of Alexander work thrilled the audience and at the same time conveyed the style and world of the play.

The three years that Jean-Louis, Pam, and I worked on this painful, haunting, hopeful play was pure joy. It went on to move audiences for two years in New York and then across the United States, The National Theatre in London, and finally The Baxter Theatre in South Africa.

It was never about success, for we had no idea that would happen. It was the exquisite experience of creating, working through the play, as each character changed, sometimes in mid-sentence, into someone else. This was accomplished as Pam's weight shifted, as did her arms, torso, head, and posture, along with her voice and accents. This was a class in and of itself, exploring each of the 23 human beings' personal behavior. This experience was the perfect example of the wonder of the Alexander Technique, for without it this play would not have been possible.

As you read each chapter of *Back to the Body*, it will awaken your body, mind, and senses to the profound meaning of being alive, the intense gradations of emotions, and the behaviors that are born from this journey. This fills the audience with the sky, sea, animals, smells, textures, and magic of sensing another human being. Now, more than ever, we need to cherish the absolute miracle of being awake and alive in our bodies, and that is the work you will discover in *Back to the Body*.

Larry Moss
New York, August 2022

INTRODUCTION

Heath Ledger as the Joker in *The Dark Knight* entering the gangster's den. Meryl Streep as Miranda Priestly in *The Devil Wears Prada* walking into the office and tossing her fur coat onto the desk. Daniel Day-Lewis in *Lincoln* picking up his sleeping child. Viola Davis as Ma Rainey in *Ma Rainey's Black Bottom*, standing her ground with a cop. Why do you remember these moments? Why do you remember these images so vividly? What is it that gives you a clear sense of who these characters are within their world and their story? The answer is simple: incredible acting through the use of the body.

Clockwise from Top Left: Meryl Streep as Miranda Priestly in
The Devil Wears Prada (2006), *Heath Ledger as the Joker in* The Dark Knight
(2008), *Daniel Day-Lewis as Abraham Lincoln in* Lincoln (2012), *and*
Viola Davis as Ma Rainey in Ma Rainey's Black Bottom (2020).
These actors create memorable characters through the use of their bodies.
(Photo Credits Clockwise from Top Left: Fox 2000 Pictures,
Licensed by: Warner Bros. Entertainment Inc. All rights reserved, Touchstone, Netflix.)

This book explores how actors can use their bodies, in concert with their voices and their emotions, in a range of roles and characters in both theatre and film. This way of working is not an abstraction, because our bodies always exist in relation to both our emotions and our environment.

Every story is told primarily through the use and expression of the actor's body. Close attention to physicality is essential to extraordinary performance, telling the story, and dealing with a character's conflicts in the most human way. The more the actor's body relates to the story, the more the audience is able to connect to the play or the film, because overcoming conflicts is a universal and inevitable human necessity.

Director and teacher Larry Moss specifically notes that "you have to discover your character's physicality and deem it as essential to your craft...Emotion unconnected to physical life doesn't reach the audience and doesn't teach them about the human being they're watching. Even if a character is physically repressed, it's the physical repression—the absence of movement—that illuminates the interior of the character."[1]

In this book, we provide a map to guide you in experiencing and using your body and its energy as a basic point of departure for performance and expression. You will learn to use your entire self in acting, involving your voice, body, mind, and emotion. This training is integrated and is designed to bring all these elements of yourself together with your material, the environment, and other actors.

The book is not a philosophy or theory book. Although there is philosophy and theory in it, each part includes explorations and hands-on work you may do on your own and with others. You will learn how you can best fill the space, serve the story, and create a unique, honest, believable, and riveting character.

Characters in stories, plays, and films are rarely balanced, harmonious people. Audiences, and our society in general, are interested in out-of-balance characters, who are more interesting, dramatically involving, and entertaining. We can connect with a flawed individual because it is more human, and we have empathy for someone trying to overcome their problems. Before you can play an unbalanced character, however, you must be able to find balance and an awareness of who you are physically. You must develop the ability to tune yourself to your physical body and use it in a way that serves the story and the character.

To achieve this balance, the actor must develop the following qualities:

- Awareness
- Buoyancy
- Weightlessness and freedom

---

[1] Larry Moss, *The Intent to Live: Achieving Your True Potential as an Actor*, Bantam Books, 2005.

- Centering

- Release of tension

- Organic breathing

- Connectedness to oneself, the story, the environment, and others

One of the best ways to achieve this balance, and more, is to understand and apply something called the Alexander Technique to your work as an actor. The Alexander Technique—named after its originator, Frederick Matthias Alexander—is a simple, powerful tool to help you develop awareness of yourself in your performance as well as in your daily life. It enables you to use your body more mindfully, free of tension and restrictive habits. In addition, it provides you with the skills to harness all your energies to create a character and live the story. This technique has been used to integrate actors' bodies and voices with their mental and emotional lives for more than 100 years in major conservatories and universities around the world.

By applying the principles laid out in this book, you will learn to use the Alexander Technique in conjunction with other ways of working to understand your character's place and role in the story and connect the material, your voice, and your spirit to your body. You will make new discoveries that endow you with an enhanced level of performance and depth.

HOW THIS BOOK IS STRUCTURED AND HOW TO USE IT

Back to the Body: Infusing Physical Life into Characters in Theatre and Film is practical and simple to use, regardless of your level of experience and whether you work in theatre, film, new media, online, or other realms. No matter how you have worked in the past or what your training is, all the information and explorations may be applied to many media and genres.

This book is divided into four main sections:

- **PART I, "THE ALEXANDER TECHNIQUE AND THE ACTOR":** This part introduces you to the Alexander Technique as a fundamental tool for all your acting work, connecting the four parts of yourself (your voice, body, mind, and heart) to the material, the story, the environment, and your performance.

- **PART II, "WHOLENESS: EXPANDING AWARENESS OF THE SELF":** This part focuses on being in the space, relating to objects, and relating to others.

- **PART III, "APPROACHING THE SCRIPT THROUGH CHARACTER":** This part teaches you how to enter the world of the story through your character and successfully create a living, breathing human being.

- **PART IV, "INTEGRATING COSTUMES, PROPS, AND SETS WITH YOUR VISION OF THE CHARACTER":** This part discusses in depth the use of costumes and props as tools to further define and embellish your character.

The book also includes a conclusion, with additional strategies to make the knowledge you have gained accessible, useful, and applicable to your work and your life on a daily basis.

Finally, it includes a series of appendixes, for extended study:

- **APPENDIX A, "THE FUTURE IS HERE: NEW TECHNOLOGIES"**

- **APPENDIX B, "FULL AND PARTIAL WARMUPS"**

- **APPENDIX C, "EXCERPTS FROM INTERVIEWS"**

The book is structured in this manner because this model of training, practice, and performance is based on the use of the self and the body and the premise that the body needs a certain process to work for you.

We encourage you to read the book in sequence because the information and explorations are laid out in a specific progression of discovery and development. That being said, if you are working on a specific role or grappling with a specific requirement (for example, you must create a relationship with a particular prop or inform the character's environment), there are certain procedures to get you there, and we have made it easy for you to look up challenge-specific exercises or approaches.

To better understand the application of these explorations to acting in both theatre and film, we highly recommend you take time to study certain films that we feel are powerful examples of masters of their craft using these concepts in their work. Throughout the book we suggest specific films we think you should watch and the concept or exploration that we think the film exemplifies or is connected to.

PART I

THE ALEXANDER TECHNIQUE AND THE ACTOR

All actors approach the work of acting with elements of themselves: their history, perception of the world, sensibility, judgments, preferences, prejudices, and most of all their habits. Our daily life and creative work are often affected by unconscious psychophysical behaviors that have developed over a lifetime. These habitual behaviors, regardless of whether you are aware of them or not, drive how you respond to and move in every activity. These habits are deeply ingrained in your nervous system and must be explored.

The culture in which we live also affects us powerfully. The overwhelming stimuli and frenetic tempo of contemporary life deeply affect our nervous systems. Most problematic are the ingrained beliefs and ways of living held deep within our DNA.

Actors must be free of these restrictions, habits, and artificial social behaviors, which tend to limit and constrain the full ability of expression. Before you can alter or change these restrictive habitual patterns, however, you must first identify and recognize them. These everyday habits might include, for example:

- Unknowingly shaking hands with new acquaintances harder than you mean to

- Gasping for air before speaking

- Collapsing the whole spine when sitting down

Lacking awareness of your body in daily activities, like sitting, can negatively affect your body.

These habits don't just affect our everyday lives; when acting, they interfere with authentic, honest performance.

You must accept the responsibility of identifying and becoming aware of these habits without bias, judgment, or shame. Recognizing and acknowledging that you have a specific habit does not necessarily mean you have to change it; it simply gives you the time and choice to do so. Once you learn to embrace all of who you are, you can discover what is getting in your way.

Frederick Matthias Alexander (1869–1955) created the Alexander Technique. He discovered the principles of his technique through his efforts to solve a vocal problem that had plagued him in his early career as an actor in Australia. Fellow actors and friends pointed out what they believed might be the cause of this problem. One told him "I can see you contracting your neck and pushing down on your body and lifting your toes off the ground," and another said that "During that Hamlet speech, I could hear you gasping for air as if you were choking."

Frederick Matthias Alexander, creator of the Alexander Technique.
(Photo: © Society of Teachers of the Alexander Technique.)

It took nine years for Alexander to develop the principles of his technique, painstakingly going through a process of self-exploration. By placing mirrors all around his studio, he was able to observe his behavior and how he moved and breathed, seeing not what he thought he was doing, but what he was *actually* doing. This began his journey of self–reeducation and was the basis for the creation of the Alexander Technique.

The Alexander Technique is the most direct and efficient system for teaching yourself how to connect with your body. It encourages you to move and behave in a way free of habits, allowing you to be present in any given circumstance, scene, and relationship, thus creating a living reality in performance. The Alexander Technique can empower you in both your personal and artistic life.

At the core of this training is reeducating the *primary control* (the relationship of the head to the spine) and a releasing and lengthening of the spine, which result in ease of function and movement. Creating a sense of ease in your work will not only clarify the character, it will give your performance a more seamless and cohesive arc.

This part of the book will guide you through the basic principles of the Alexander Technique: awareness, inhibition, primary control, and direction. It also discusses breath coordination and the voice. It does this through procedures and explorations to give you first-hand experience with this technique.

AWARENESS

In the Alexander Technique, *awareness* means becoming conscious of yourself in time and space. It refers to how we use our mind in relationship to our body and how we respond to action.

When stimulated or confronted by anything, we never respond just physically or only mentally. Our immediate and honest response is integrated—a unified physical and mental reaction. It also encompasses an awareness of our anatomy because our energy is crucial in using our body with the greatest amount of ease, flexibility, and power.

The Alexandrian definition of awareness includes the possibility of making changes in the process of action. Reaching a goal is a constant flow of intermediary steps that are as important as achieving the goal itself. Awareness of your whole body in action, and consideration of how you use your body in action (free, tense, or coordinated), affects the creative journey you take toward achieving your goals. Having awareness enables you to make choices in the moment to tell the story in the most effective, believable, and expressive way possible.

AVOID END-GAINING

It is human nature to want to find the right answer or achieve what you perceive to be the desired result as quickly as possible. But by making mistakes, you often learn more than by getting it "right" immediately.

In everything that we will ask you to do, in this part and throughout the book, we are more concerned that you explore and experience the moment-to-moment elements than take shortcuts or rush to get to the final result—something Alexander called *end-gaining*.

End-gaining bypasses the learning process and deprives you of the opportunity to make new discoveries and choices. It often produces tension, anxiety, and a stereotypical response. It also usually results in bad acting—indicating, telegraphing, and literalism—rather than outcomes that are inventive, authentic, and rich. In both your work and your daily life, your journey is often more important than your destination!

End-gaining will not help you win the race.

Whereas a musician, for example, has an instrument to play, as an actor, you have only yourself. When we talk about the *self*, we are not merely talking about an idea. We are talking about your entire being—your whole self. This is not just an intellectual construct or concept. The whole self is your body, your mind, your voice, and your heart (or soul or spirit—whatever that intangible thing is that makes you who you are). Awareness is the starting point for accessing and maximizing your whole instrument.

EXPLORATION: CONSTRUCTIVE REST

To develop awareness, we invite you to explore the integrated use of your mind and body by practicing the constructive rest or semi-supine exploration. Be mindful of using both as you begin this exploration. The goal is to help you view yourself as a physical map as you calmly and clearly explore your body's geography.

> **NOTE:** When we teach these explorations, we compare your body to the house that you live in. Often, we are more familiar with some rooms, while others go unused and ignored. All the "rooms" of your body need to be explored and integrated to harness the full power and awareness of your being.

This exploration is one of Alexander's fundamental, simple procedures to connect with yourself, rid yourself of unnecessary tensions, and organize yourself. This exploration is a valuable way to begin any warmup and prepare for rehearsal or performance. Our students have told us that whenever they do this—whether it is before an audition, a rehearsal, or performance, or afterward, as a cooldown to help release the accumulated emotional and physical tension of a performance—it centers them, creates awareness, and unifies their bodies, minds, and emotions.

The whole process should take between 15 and 20 minutes. It is set up like a musical phrase that works only if played fluidly from beginning to end, so the effectiveness of this exploration will be adversely affected if you read a step, attempt it, read the next step, continue, and so on.

It might be wise the first few times you attempt this exploration to listen to and be guided by the voice on the MP3 recording that will be available to you on the *Back to the Body* website at https://alexandertechworks.com/back-to-the-body/. This reflects a specific way of positively inviting your mind and body to explore without judgment and without attempting to achieve the "right" result. Remember, this is not about fixing anything. It is about discovering where you are in your mind and body, without worry or fear of doing it "correctly." This is awareness in movement, awareness in activity.

SETUP

There are two ways of proceeding with this exploration. If you are in a group, one person should read the instructions aloud as the others perform them; if you are alone, listen to the audio and let it guide you.

You will need a hard foam mat, half an inch thick. This thickness is preferred because standard yoga mats don't give enough support to the back, and the tailbone often becomes uncomfortable. You will also need between two and four paperback books to support your head, depending on the length and shape of your spine.

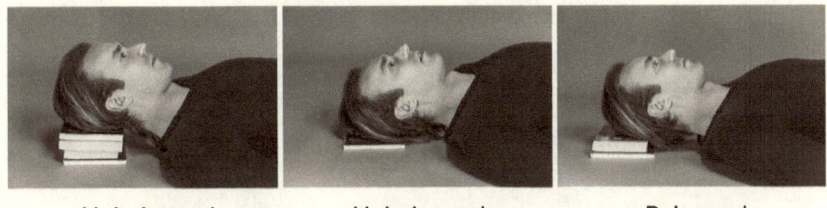

Unbalanced   Unbalanced   Balanced

Too many books will force your neck to constrict in the front.
Too few will pull your head back and down. (Photo: Todd Domenic Cribari.)

NOTE: Do not use these photos to count the number of books necessary to achieve balance. Everyone is different. These photos are for reference, only.

EXPLORATION

1. Lie down on the mat with a couple of paperback books under your head, right on the occipital bone, located at the bottom of the skull before it descends to the rest of the neck (the atlanto-occipital joint). The number of books you use depends on the tension of your neck and the curve and length of your spine. Start by putting a couple of books under your head. If your neck is stretched too straight and your chin is too close to your chest, you have too many books. If the back of your neck is contracted and your chin is pointed toward the ceiling, you probably do not have enough. The goal is to provide enough support for the head so that it is balanced at the top of the spine.

2. Bend your knees, with your feet flat on the ground, heels hip-width apart. Place your hands on your stomach, not touching each other, with your elbows bent and resting at your sides. This will help you release the tension in your shoulders and experience width in your back.

The body in a state of balance in constructive rest.
(Photo: Todd Domenic Cribari.)

3. Gently pressing your feet down, peel your sacrum (the triangular bone at the base of the spine just below the fifth lumbar vertebra) from the floor, raising your pelvis up toward the ceiling.

4. Once your pelvis is raised, place the palms of your hands underneath your buttocks. Then, breathing out, gently lower your pelvis vertebra by vertebra, using your hands to guide your pelvis away from your head as you lower it to the ground. As you allow your spine to lengthen on the mat, do not stiffen your neck. Your main objective is to allow something to happen, rather than pushing or forcing it to happen.

Think of your breaths as waves of water moving through you. By breathing like this, you become more aware of the map of your whole body.

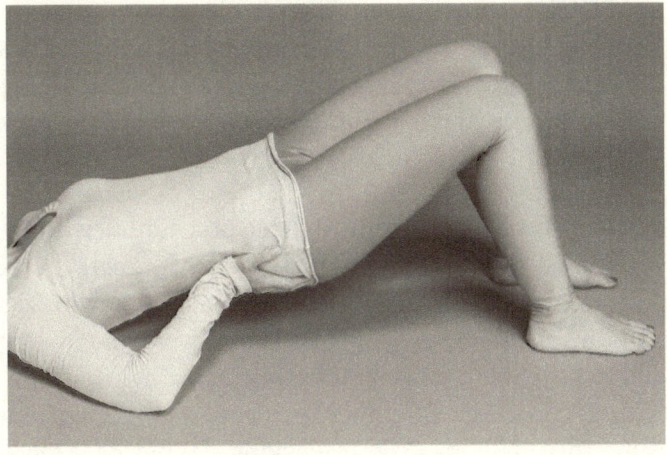

Hand position on the pelvis to direct it away from the head.
(Photo: Todd Domenic Cribari.)

5. As you are lying in this position, allow gravity to release your torso even further into the mat. Gravity and the floor will become your best friends as you observe yourself from the top of your head to your lower back. Include your arms and legs in this awareness.

6. Wherever you are in your breathing cycle, allow a sigh to flow out as you whisper "AHHHHH" (the most open vowel). Feel the vibration of the breath and sound moving through your whole body. Continue letting each breath come out on an "AH." Do not push to take large, deep inhalations of breath. As you focus on the exhalation of the whispered "AH," your body will automatically take in the breath you need.

You might notice that some breaths are larger than others, just as some ocean waves are larger than others. These currents of breath will continue to massage your internal viscera (all the organs and soft tissues inside your body).

You might also notice areas of tension and bundles of muscular contractions, or even whole areas of your body that seem absent. Do not try to shift, fix, or compensate for these areas. Instead, allow your breath to enter these centers of tension.

NOTE: Again, this is not a time for fixing things. It is a time for taking stock, with the intent of noticing where the tension is and seeing if, with each exhalation and inhalation, breathing and gravity will help everything shift and settle organically. Remember, what you do not feel about yourself is as important as what you do feel.

7. After you spend 15 to 20 minutes lying down, notice that you have a clearer understanding of your body map. Although you might not have a picture of every nook and cranny, you likely have a better connection to your body. The goal is to develop a curiosity of the self and to be willing to live in the question rather than the answer. Every time you observe yourself, you are encouraging your senses to attune to your body. You are asking, "What do I feel? What's going on? Where am I in my body?"

8. To transition to a standing position, lengthen as you gently roll your head either to the left or right, allowing the whole body to follow, so you end up lying on your side. Pause and breathe, finding ease in that position.

9. Leading with your head, continue to roll until you are on your hands and knees. Release your head slightly forward and away from your spine, so your head is not retracting back and down.

CAUTION: If you have any knee or hip issues, do not attempt the next step.

10. Bring your head forward toward the floor so it is supported by the mat and sit back with your pelvis on your heels in child's pose (in yoga, *balasana*). Keep your arms at your sides to help release your shoulders. This is a very relaxing position that allows the weight of your head to be supported by the floor, as well as allowing your spine to lengthen as you breathe into your lower back.

11. Like a snake, starting with the sacral area, slowly uncurl your body one vertebra at a time. Release the neck and let your head hang, working your way up until you are on your knees with your head perched at the top of the spine. Gaze straight ahead to the farthest horizon.

12. Gently allow your head to lead your whole body up, putting your weight on one foot and then the other, and slowly bring yourself to a standing position. Take a moment to notice the balance of your whole body weight on your feet, feeling the same awareness of yourself that you felt when you were on the floor.

13. Leading with your head, allowing it to move away from your spine in an upward direction, slowly walk around the room, observing the map of yourself as you move.

> **NOTE:** When we say "leading with your head," we do not mean that your head is jutting forward in front of your body, but that your head is causing your spine to lengthen as you move around the room.

REFLECTION

- What did you notice when you first settled on the mat with the books under your head?

- Did you notice any areas of tension or imbalanced weight? How did this change as gravity caused your body to spread?

- Did one side of your body feel longer or heavier than the other?

- Did the areas of tension or discomfort change throughout the procedure?

- Did you feel more comfortable as you continued breathing?

- As you were exploring, did you feel any emotions in your body? Was there any fear?

- Did you experience contractions or tingling sensations?

- Was it challenging to notice what was going on in your body without trying to change it? Or were you able to notice and be aware of what was going on in your body without trying to alter, fix, or adjust?

- Once you were standing, were you still present in your body? Were you able to sustain the awareness as you stood up and walked?

- How do you feel now that you have finished this process? Be specific. Remember, there are not any right or wrong answers. The purpose of this reflection is to be aware of what you felt while doing this exploration.

INHIBITION: "I HAVE TIME"

"Between what happened to him, or the stimulus, and his response to it, was his freedom or power to choose that response."

–Stephen R. Covey, on psychiatrist Victor Frankl,
Holocaust survivor and author of *Man's Search for Meaning*

We always have a choice when responding to the stimuli in our lives. The most effective way to respond is by using inhibition. When we say *inhibition*, we are not talking about Freudian inhibition—restricting, restraining, or shutting down—but rather Alexander's definition: the ability to take time to choose the manner in which you respond.

According to the Alexander Technique, inhibition means taking enough time to study your situation and find the best possible course of action in relation to your goals. It is creating enough space between stimulus and response so that you may make a choice that is not based on an automatic response or habit.

For an actor, this idea of taking time before responding is a fundamental process that should be learned and applied to acting. It can literally change the quality of a scene or moment, helping the actor to clarify the objectives of the character and to serve the author's vision. By delaying your initial, instantaneous response to any stimulus, whether that response is learned or instinctive, you may discover new choices, a better use of yourself, and less tension in the action in which you are engaging.

WITHOUT INHIBITION

WITH INHIBITION

Applying inhibition will help you avoid disaster.

The choices you make in how you respond as an actor are vital to your communication in both everyday life and performance. There is incredible power in saying to yourself, "I have time," before going into any performance or activity. This principle may be used in all facets of your process as an actor. Before you begin a class, go in for an audition, or start a rehearsal, you should stop, literally say, "I have time," and take the time to release your neck, lengthen and widen your body, and connect with your breath. This will make an enormous difference in the quality of your work.

NOTE: "I have time." This simple phrase, said out loud, not only has the power to affect your work as an actor, but can also deeply affect how you navigate through your life during times of stress.

Some actors use inhibition as a foundation of their work. Sir Ben Kingsley and Dame Judi Dench are famous for their use of inhibition and their ability to convey power through the economy of movement. In *Sexy Beast* (2000), Kingsley's character, Don Logan, commands fear through inhibition rather than by being physically violent. We see the power and threat of his character within him through poise and stillness rather than through any external movements. It is the implied possibility and threat of violence that make him more terrifying than any action he actually carries out.

Ben Kingsley as Don Logan in Sexy Beast. *Kingsley is an absolute master of the economy of movement.* (20th Century Fox.)

At the end of *Skyfall* (2012), Dench, in her seventh outing as the character M, is shot. Rather than play the physical desperation and pain of being mortally wounded, she chooses inhibition. We know she is dying, as she herself does, but rather than making the obvious and easy choice of playing the pain of her imminent death—doubling over, tightening her voice, gasping for breath—she maintains her stature and power in her final moments.

SCOTT

In 2007, I directed a cue script production of *Twelfth Night*. This is a method duplicating the rehearsal process (or lack thereof) that was used in the late 16th century at the Globe Theatre, wherein actors would neither read the entire play nor rehearse with the other actors until the opening night performance in front of an audience. Instead, they would make their choices based only on their character's text.

Five days before the opening-night performance, the actors suddenly realized they were on the verge of performing a play they had never rehearsed. The entire company was in a high state of anxiety and fear. Jean-Louis told them, "Say these words out loud: 'I have time.'" They did. Instantly, before our eyes, they transformed. The tension was drained from the room. Their faces and bodies visibly relaxed. There was a sense of peace, calm, and empowerment. They could get back to work with focus and energy.

NOTE: Making the choice *not* to perform an action can be as powerful as performing the action!

WATCH THESE MOVIES:
BRIDGE OF SPIES (2015) AND *WOLF HALL* (2015)

Despite the difference in period, genre, and character, as Thomas Cromwell in *Wolf Hall* and as Rudolf Abel in *Bridge of Spies*, Mark Rylance uses inhibition to convey so much while doing so little. There is great power in the calm and stillness of both these characters.

Mark Rylance as Thomas Cromwell in Wolf Hall.
Through inhibition, Rylance conveyed his intent to the audience while masking his feelings from the other characters.
(BBC Worldwide.)

EXPLORATION: BASIC CONCEPT OF INHIBITION

There are simple actions you do many times every day without stopping to think about them: locking the door when you leave the house, picking up a pen, opening up your laptop, shaking someone's hand, or just standing up from a chair. This exploration will help you understand how inhibition can influence how you move and respond when doing even the most pedestrian tasks.

> **NOTE:** When you receive and process stimuli, whether you end up reacting or not, the nervous system is acting in the same way. It is still firing messages to your body to react. The dynamic moment is when you decide to proceed with the action or not.

When your nervous system has an impulse and sends a message to your body to react, you have the choice to use inhibition. You have time.

SETUP

You will need a chair. You can do this working with a partner or in a group with someone leading the exploration.

EXPLORATION

1. Sit upright in a chair with your feet flat on the floor.

2. Come forward on the chair and sit on the rounded bones at the very end of your pelvis (the ischial tuberosity; we will call them your "sits bones"). You can find them by putting your hands under your buttocks while you're sitting and rocking slightly forward and backward in your chair, keeping your feet flat on the ground. One way to picture them is as the "feet" of the spine.

17

NOTE: Many people sit too far back on their sits bones, causing them to collapse the front of their torsos, thus causing their abdomens to protrude. Others are pitched too far forward on the sits bones, causing them to arch the lower back, lifting and stiffening the ribcage. Human beings are designed to balance squarely on the middle of their sits bones, using them as support.

3. Stand up and sit back down quickly. Do this four times without stopping. What did you notice about this action? How did you feel?

   Perhaps you felt winded, tense, or stressed. You might even have found the action difficult.

4. Repeat step 3, but this time, before you stand up, pause and say out loud, "I have time." After you stand, pause again and say, "I have time," then sit back down. Do this four times.

   This time, when performing the action with inhibition, you were likely able to perform the same action with less effort and exertion, with a sense of ease in your movement. In using inhibition, you created space between your intent and your action, which allowed you greater clarity, less tension, and the opportunity to coordinate the whole body and mind.

REFLECTION

- How did that feel? What did you notice the second time?
- Was there a difference in the quality of the movement and in how you felt after you finished?

EXPLORATION: FOLLOWING COMMANDS

In this exploration, you will follow a series of commands.

SETUP

You will need a chair. You can do this working with a partner or in a group with someone leading the exploration.

EXPLORATION

1. Sit upright in a chair with your feet flat on the floor.

2. As your partner calls out commands to you, follow each command.

   Partner: Stand up.

   Sit down.

   Stand up.

   Raise your right hand up in the air.

   Put your hand down.

   Scream.

   Take three steps forward.

   Take three steps backward.

   Sit back down in the chair.

3. Go through this same process again with your partner calling out the exact same commands. However, this time, do not follow the commands and do not respond at all.

4. Switch places with your partner and repeat the exercise.

REFLECTION

- Did you notice a difference between the first time, when you were following the commands, and the second time, when you were not?

- What did you notice the second time? How did you feel?

- When you heard the commands, although you made the choice to inhibit, did you still feel the impulse to perform the actions?

- Did you feel your muscles tensing in anticipation of the actions? Did you visualize yourself performing the action?

- Did you feel a sense of space and peace? Or did you feel suppressed and find it difficult to not follow the command?

Hopefully, when doing this last exploration, you felt, in your body, that making the choice *not* to perform an action can be as powerful as performing the action!

> *"Often, to refrain from an act is no less an act than to commit one, because inhibition is co-equally with excitation a nervous activity."*
>
> –Sir Charles Sherrington, Nobel Prize–winning physiologist

PRIMARY CONTROL

Primary control refers to the relationship of the head to the body and how that crucial relationship can be used effectively (or ineffectively) in your everyday activities as well as in performance. The key tenet of primary control is that the most efficient way of moving is with the head leading upward and the spine following, thereby lengthening and widening your entire body.

In our everyday lives, whenever we move, we habitually compress and apply pressure to our spines by pulling our heads back and down, pressing down on the joints through our hips, knees, and ankles. This results in tight, inefficient, heavy movement when standing, sitting, and walking.

But if you think of your spine as a spring, and you relieve the pressure from the top of your head, this upward redirection allows the pressure to begin to release. This creates a better distribution of effort and weight throughout the whole body, encouraging buoyancy and radiating all the way down through the joints. Moving in this manner releases pressure and constriction, allowing you to effortlessly move more efficiently and effectively.

*We often forget to be aware of how we use our bodies in our daily activities.
Notice how we have a tendency to bring our heads forward and
down and collapse our spines.*

*When your head goes forward and up, your body is balanced and aligned,
enabling you to move effortlessly and efficiently.*
(Photo: Todd Domenic Cribari.)

We start out moving like this when we first walk, as children, with our heads and bodies in perfect balance. As we get older, tension, stress, and the accumulation of bad habits interfere with this balance, adversely affecting our ability to connect to ourselves. Restoring this balance is the key to enabling yourself to move and connect to the world and the people around you with clarity, purpose, and freedom.

In the animal world, all the senses are located in the head. When moving its head, an animal is always orienting itself in space, scanning the environment for food or danger—for example, smelling the scent of a predator. This alert sensory activity animates the relationship between the head and the spine, which is why it is almost impossible to find any kind of animal with a stiff neck or poor posture. It is this function of relating to the environment that inevitably brings about the effective use of the animal.

We can all learn from the meerkat—the perfect example of a balanced body poised for action! (Photo: Getty Images.)

EXPLORATION: HEAD, RIBCAGE, PELVIS

When you allow the head to lead the body upward, it helps the whole spine to lengthen, creating freedom through the joints and allowing a distribution of effort through your whole body. In this exploration, you will coordinate and connect your head to your entire body, in action. Practicing this way of moving in your daily life, as well as in your work as an actor, will promote a more efficient use of your body and a feeling of general well-being.

SETUP

You will need an open space large enough to move around in. You can do this working alone or in a group. Remind yourself that you have time.

> **NOTE:** You should begin every exploration by reminding yourself that you have time. This is accomplished by literally saying, out loud, "I have time." Say it slowly, hear yourself say it, and believe it.

EXPLORATION

1. Stand on your feet, hip-width apart, with your weight evenly distributed on your heels and the balls of your feet. Make sure your feet are parallel to each other, with your big toe and first and second toes facing forward. Remind yourself that you have time.

2. Free your neck to allow your head to go forward and up. This enables your whole body to lengthen and widen and your knees to go forward. Continue this process of directing your body as you perform this exploration.

3. Place your hands on the side of your head, palms at the hinge of your jaws, and say, "This is my head."

JEAN-LOUIS

A few years ago, I taught a class of young musicians—5- to 10-year-old musical prodigies. Because of their long hours of disciplined, regimented practice, with little or no playtime, they had already developed stiffness and tension while playing their instruments.

I wanted them to understand the relationship between their heads and bodies. Normally, I would have used my hands on them to give them a kinesthetic awareness of how they were using their bodies. Due to their age, however, I was asked by their mothers to please refrain from any physical contact with their children. I was a little thrown by this, for without physically touching them, how could I get these children to understand how to use their bodies?

After much thought, I created a game I called "Head-Ribcage-Pelvis" to enable them to connect to their bodies and create an ease of movement in themselves. First, I had them put their hands on the side of their heads, with their palms at the hinge of their jaws, and say, "This is my head." Then, they put their hands on the side of their lower ribcage, and said, "This is my ribcage." Finally, they put their hands on the side of their hips, with their palms on their ball-and-socket joint, and said, "This is my pelvis." I asked them to repeat the exercise sequentially, without stopping, saying, "Head, ribcage, pelvis, head, ribcage, pelvis, head, ribcage, pelvis." They walked around the room, repeating these words and the placement of their hands, faster and faster. This process connected the separate parts into a coordinated whole.

After completing this exercise, the musicians sat down to play their instruments. Their playing was not only flawless and fluid, but I could see an improvement in the manner of their playing and a relaxation and breath in their music, as they were now allowing their energy and effort to be evenly distributed throughout the whole structure of their bodies.

4. Move your hands to the side of your lower ribcage and say, "This is my ribcage."

5. Put your hands on the side of your hips, palms on your ball-and-socket joint, and say, "This is my pelvis."

6. Repeat this process two more times, placing your hands on your head, then your ribcage, then your pelvis, while saying, "this is my head, this is my ribcage, this is my pelvis".

7. Walk around the room as you say "Head, ribcage, pelvis, head, ribcage, pelvis," speaking and moving more and more rapidly as you go. As you do, envision these parts of the body as one connected whole.

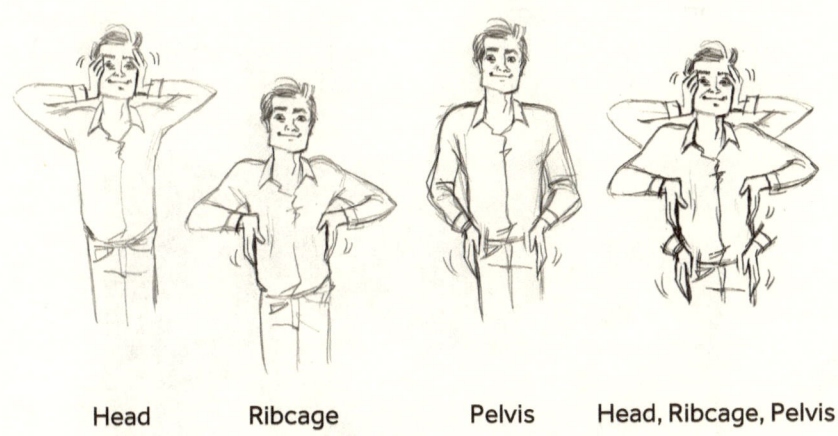

Head   Ribcage   Pelvis   Head, Ribcage, Pelvis

The Head-Ribcage-Pelvis game.

NOTE: As you perform this exercise, make sure that as you move faster, you bring your hands up to your head, rather than pull your head down into your hands. Lengthen and widen your body as you connect to your head, ribcage, and pelvis.

8. Continue walking but stop doing the hand movements. As you are walking, notice what is different and how your body feels.

REFLECTION

- How do you feel at the end of this process?

- Take a few steps. Do you feel lighter while walking? Do you feel a different coordination in your body in the act of walking? Do you feel freer? Are you distributing your effort more evenly as you are walking?

WATCH THIS MOVIE:
SOPHIE'S CHOICE (1982)

While at Juilliard, the Alexander Technique classes were Kevin Kline's favorite part of his training. You can see how he exquisitely applies primary control throughout his performance. Pay close attention to his use of himself during the toasting scene on the bridge.

Kevin Kline as Nathan in Sophie's Choice. *As he conducts an imaginary orchestra, Kline exemplifies the concept of primary control.*
(Universal Pictures.)

DIRECTION

Now that you understand the principles of awareness, primary control, and inhibition, we can integrate the process of direction. The Alexandrian definition of *direction* is the ability to conduct energy to the mechanisms of the body responsible for everyday movement and skilled activities, to enable you to move, with ease, in the most effective way.

Standing, walking, and sitting are activities we engage in daily. They are the basis of every physical activity. Awareness of how you move when standing, walking, and sitting in your everyday life can be a powerful tool in improving your use of your body, both as an actor and as a person.

Many actors build their characters by first discovering how their characters do these three activities. They spend a great deal of time experimenting and practicing their gait, rhythm, shape, balance of weight, intensity, and urgency. We are not saying you must figure this out from the beginning, but knowing how your character sits, stands, and walks can act as a physical foundation from which you can continue to build the character.

You have been walking, sitting, and standing your entire life, and you have inevitably developed ingrained ways of doing these things. Choosing a direction enables you to alter your habitual way of moving. By using the principles of inhibition and direction, you may change the subconscious habits of a lifetime to make a conscious choice of how your character moves.

Direction enables you to prepare your mind and body to go into action. To help you evenly distribute your effort along the whole of your body, Alexander developed a sequence of directions. This sequence of directions is constant and fluid, like breathing. Alexander's directions are a way of thinking in action. You are aiming yourself in a particular way that not only promotes an improved state of being but also helps you in creating a character. Although we are going to guide you through this sequence one step after another, think of it as one fluid and connected movement that occurs almost simultaneously.

ALEXANDER'S SEQUENCE OF DIRECTIONS

Allow your neck to be free...

To allow your head to go forward and up...

To allow your body to lengthen and widen...

To allow your knees to go forward and away...

To allow your feet to go into the ground...

One after another, all together

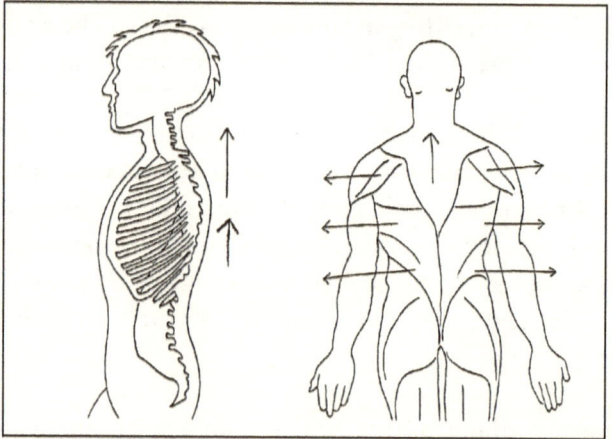

Alexander's sequence of directions encourages you to lengthen and widen.
(Drawings: David Gorman, Left; John Nichols, Right.)

NOTE: We will address how to use direction to create a character and tell a story in the chapters to come.

JEAN-LOUIS

I worked with Leonardo DiCaprio to develop his character for J. Edgar Hoover in *J. Edgar.* DiCaprio wanted Hoover to walk through the world with precision, as if he were a predatory creature who owned his territory.

DiCaprio found a way of walking with intensity, each step that he took communicating that he was the head of the FBI, watching everyone like a hawk, testing everyone for strength and weakness of character. In contrast, DiCaprio's habitual walk was relaxed and casual.

Once DiCaprio found Hoover's walk, he practiced it for hours and hours over a period of weeks until it became second nature to him. He was filmed, during the costume and makeup tests, practicing his walk and mannerisms in full costume and makeup. We would watch these tests together, fine-tuning and making sure that there was consistency in Hoover's physical behavior.

Through this process, DiCaprio eradicated his old way of walking and found a new walk, which he used as a foundation for refining other elements of the character. In addition, he mastered the physicality and rhythm to get to the point where Hoover's walk was seamless and authentic.

WATCH THIS MOVIE: *J. Edgar* (2011)

The consistency with which DiCaprio alters his physical behavior and movement throughout his portrayal of Hoover's life is an excellent example of an actor using direction in a performance. It gave him the ability to maintain continuity in his character's behavior as he aged as Hoover, over the years, in the film.

Leonardo DiCaprio as J. Edgar Hoover in J. Edgar. *DiCaprio's use of direction while walking or, as in this scene, reviewing his agents, gave his character a steely purpose throughout the story.*

EXPLORATION: DIRECTION

In this exploration, you will imagine your spine as a strand of pearls lying on a table. If you pick up the first pearl, the rest of the strand will follow, one after another, all together. This exploration of direction may be used both when you move and when you are still to help you understand and experience direction at rest and in movement. Feel free to move your body as you go through this exploration. The movement will be gentle and easy because this is a directional thought, rather than a muscular action.

SETUP

This exploration requires a space that is large enough for people to move around freely. If you are doing the exercise alone, you do not need much space, but if there are many people, you should be in a studio with enough room for everyone to move around without feeling constricted or worrying about running into each other.

EXPLORATION

1. Stand as you normally would—as if you were waiting for a bus. Say "I have time." What do you notice about how you are standing? Do not alter how you are standing; just observe and notice.

   - Are your head and neck jutting forward?

   - Is your weight on one leg or is it distributed evenly on both your feet?

   - Is one shoulder higher or lower than the other?

   - Are you collapsed on the top of your spine with your chest caved in?

   - Is your pelvis pushed forward?

   - Do you feel heavy?

If the answer to any of these questions is yes, don't worry. This is how most of us stand when we are in stillness. Let's explore how we can use the Alexander Technique to find greater ease and balance in our posture at rest.

2. As you are standing, allow your neck to release, your head to go forward and up, your torso to lengthen and widen, and your knees to release forward and out toward your big toes, with your feet engaged and grounded.

Notice that we use the word *allow* to link each step. This is an important part of the Alexander Technique because both the intent and physical aspect of each step release and connect to the whole person. The goal is to bring directional thought into a specific sequence of actions that integrate the body. You are allowing and facilitating a natural sequence of events that give you the most coordinated and free use of yourself.

3. Observe how your weight is distributed. You might want to experiment with this. For example, allow the front of your ankles to release. Explore bringing the weight forward on the balls of your feet and then slightly backward onto your heels, finding the place where your weight is balanced and distributed evenly between them. Do not stiffen; move your head, looking left and looking right, shifting the balance of your body from your ankles up.

> **NOTE:** You are not trying to lock onto the "right" stance; you simply want to feel the act of balancing and fluidity, the coordination of your whole body in the action of standing.

4. Now that you have used direction to feel comfortable standing, walk around the room. Notice what happens and how you feel. Try to maintain the comfort and balance you had standing while you are moving.

Most people, even though they have just found a lighter self while standing, revert to their habitual walk once they start moving. They may walk heavily and stiffly, their spine and head more collapsed, their hips forward and down. As they walk, they think of stepping down on each step, which encourages a shuffle or waddle.

5. Let's try this again. Stand still and repeat the steps you did before. Allow your neck to release, your head to go forward and up, your torso to lengthen and widen, and your knees to release forward and out toward your big toes, with your feet engaged and grounded. This time, as you begin to walk, continue repeating these directions. As you bend your knees, tell them to bend forward. As you go up, the foot goes down. The head leads up, the body follows—one after another, altogether—just like a string of pearls.

Assisting a student to lengthen and widen as she walks.
(Photo: Todd Domenic Cribari.)

REFLECTION

- Do you notice a difference in how you are walking now? How is your weight changing step-by-step? Are you lighter? Is your spine more lengthened as you engage in the act of walking?

- Did you find yourself trying to be pulled up by an outside force?

- Did you try to hold yourself in the "right" posture? People often fall into this trap of trying to achieve the "right" position; this is not what direction is about and will make you move stiffly.

BREATH COORDINATION AND THE VOICE

Breath is your fuel, energy, and life. As we introduce and explore breathing, we want to remind you that breathing is a natural occurrence in humans that should never be forced. You do not need to tell yourself to breathe any more than you need to tell your heart to beat. It is part of your autonomic nervous system (ANS) that regulates your breath and your circulation system.

Breathing is an automatic, reflexive activity that involves the whole body and a coordinated use of the breathing mechanism. But when you consciously take a deep breath and try to "tank up," you raise your shoulders, stiffen your ribcage, and throw your head back and down, which creates constriction and tension.

We are always either letting old breath out or allowing new breath in. As we breathe, every organ and every joint in our body is affected. When we exhale, we create a vacuum in our lungs, which is filled by an effortless inhale. While we use our muscles in the act of breathing, those muscles aid us in, but do not initiate, breathing.

Chemically, as oxygen comes in, it gives every muscle of the human body the energy to effect movement. Breathing is all about allowing the used-up breath, full of carbon dioxide (CO_2), out and letting a new breath, richer in oxygen, in. CO_2 is a byproduct of our body's life functions, which is a stressor to your nervous system. Holding your breath increases the amount of CO_2 in your body, increasing tension. Oxygen releases tension, creating more ease. Ease in the functioning of your body is essential, allowing your creative juices to flow.

Breathing is an activity of the whole torso. As humans, we are frontally oriented, meaning most of our daily focus, socially, physically, and professionally, happens in front of us. We look forward, using our hands in all kinds of activities in front of us, and we have very little thought and awareness about our backs.

Paradoxically, the back supports our arms and is responsible for distributing effort throughout our whole body. If you were a dog, a cat, or some other animal, you would be rolling on your back, rubbing or scratching it against a wall or a tree. You would have a much better relationship with your back than you do as a human. We often ignore our backs unless we are in pain.

Though we think of our lungs as being in the front of our chest, a greater portion is located in our back. That's where doctors put their stethoscopes to listen to our lungs. To find ease in our breath, we must let our sides and back expand to accommodate our lungs filling up with air. As you inhale, the diaphragm (an organ muscle that looks like an open umbrella in the middle of your ribcage) moves your ribcage slightly up and out, spreading and descending down, pushing on your viscera (all the internal organs in your abdomen), and slightly displacing them.

When you do not tense excessively, you can see your belly expand and feel the bottom of your pelvis (the pelvic floor) gently descend. As you exhale, your ribcage descends and drapes over your organs as the diaphragm starts its journey upward, pushing the air out of you and regulating the pressure. If, as you are breathing, you tense your buttocks, stiffen your ankle joints, or hyperextend your knees, you will interfere with this movement. You speak or sing on an exhale. When you exhale fully, inhaling is inevitable and automatic. You don't have to think about it; you just allow it. The amount of breath you need will change based on your emotional state or physical activity. If you are clear about what you are saying and why, your body will take enough breath to support it.

RELAXATION VERSUS EASE

We often think of relaxing as drooping and getting heavy, which is not going to serve you. So, when a director or acting teacher asks you to relax, think of that as finding ease. Being at ease is different from trying to relax. When we try to relax, we often start tensing even more or collapse our bodies and become limp like a wet noodle, without spinal support or energy. Ease, however, allows us to function with the most efficiency. It creates the internal space for our imagination, thoughts, free impulses, and emotions to occur.

LIGHT PROJECTS, SOUND REVERBERATES

When a director says, "I can't hear you. You need to project," we start to push our voice and yell, creating tension. Rather than thinking about projecting your voice, instead think about creating more resonance in your vocal mechanism.

How do you do that? Imagine you are a beautiful cello. In function, human vocal cords resemble the strings of a cello. Just as the wooden body of the cello resonates the sound, making it bigger and richer, your physical body resonates the sound you are making.

Qualities like tone, volume, fullness, warmth, or harshness inform the audience about the emotional state of your character. When your body is free of excessive tension, it will allow your emotions to be expressed through sound in a variety of shades and colors. Even when you speak quietly, you can have free, rich vibrations, with strong emotional content.

It is absolutely necessary to distribute the ease and the effort throughout your body to bring the complexity of real life into your character—especially in intimate scenes. Breathing effortlessly with your whole body will allow all of this to happen.

JEAN-LOUIS

I first met Larry Moss in 1992 in Santa Monica, where he was running an acting studio. He came to me to study the Alexander Technique because he was interested in becoming freer and more connected to his body. Having been a professional actor and singer on Broadway, Larry was willing to go all the way in terms of experimenting and applying what he was learning to his performance.

Gradually, Larry began referring many of his students to work with me. He also invited me to watch his acting classes. Visiting his class was truly a turning point in my artistic life, as well as in my personal life. It was during this period of visiting Larry's class that I first learned about his Story Exercise. For the Story Exercise, Larry would have his students partner up and give them 15 minutes or so to relax and connect to their bodies and breath. He would then instruct them to allow an event to come into their awareness. This event could have happened yesterday or 20 years ago—it doesn't matter. Finally, he told them to remember every conceivable sensory detail about the experience—how it looked, smelled, tasted, felt, and sounded—and to relive this memory with their partner.

A month later, Larry asked me to come back to class to watch the Story Exercise conducted by one of his students: a South African actress named Pamela Gien. The story she shared was about the murder of her Grandpa George, who was stabbed in the back 22 times by a Rhodesian freedom fighter. As she lived her story, she played herself as a six-year old child, as well as her father, mother, and her nanny, Salamina.

I was stunned at the depth of Pamela's story. I was also impressed with her grace and physical ability to tell the story. But I detected stiffness in her movements and interference with the transitions between one character and the other. There was tension in her body and voice that came from the challenge of playing all these characters in one body.

Morphing her body and voice from a child to an older nanny was definitely daunting. After watching Pamela's performance in the Story Exercise, I wrote her a letter with specific notes about the scene, which I also shared with Larry.

Larry asked me to work with Pamela on an ongoing basis to prepare her for what would become her award-winning play *The Syringa Tree*. I worked with Pam to help her access the natural reserve of energy in the body through her breath—specifically by lowering the center of her breath from the upper chest to the pelvis and the back of the ribs. Pam used this method of breathing both before and during the performance— as a calming mechanism, but also to gain energy in extreme moments.

It took us three full years to develop the play, with the help of producer Matt Salinger, to the point where it could be produced for the first time, in Seattle, at ACT. In 2001, *The Syringa Tree* opened at Playhouse 91 in New York. It won the Obie for the Best Off-Broadway Play, and Pamela won the Drama Desk and Outer Critics Circle Awards for Best Solo Performance of the Year. Since then, the play has been performed many times throughout the world.

Pamela Gien used the Alexander Technique to clearly define the 23 characters she played in The Syringa Tree.
(Courtesy of Catherine Ashmore, Royal National Theatre.)

EXPLORATION: FINDING EASE IN ANGER

Not paying enough attention to your breath—or, conversely, becoming obsessed with it—can only create trouble for an actor. Spend time with your breath every day. As you go through your daily life, pay attention to your breath during different activities. It's a good practice to experiment, take time, and notice how you're breathing, observing the exhalation and the quality of the breath. Although breathing is automatic, we still need to be aware of how we use our breathing apparatus and, most importantly, how we interfere with it.

SETUP

This exploration requires a space that is large enough for people to move around freely. If you are doing the exercise alone, you do not need much space, but if there are many people, you should be in a studio with enough room for everyone to move around without feeling constricted.

EXPLORATION

1. Place your feet hip-width apart, with your weight evenly distributed on your heels and the balls of your feet. Make sure your big toe and the first and second toes are pointing forward and that your feet are parallel. (A turned-out posture tightens the hips and lower back, preventing the neck from being free.) Tell yourself, "I have time." As you are standing, allow yourself to breathe fully.

2. Free your neck to allow your head to go forward and up, your whole body to lengthen and widen, and your knees to go forward. Continue this process of directing your body as you proceed.

3. Scream "NO," making the sound in your throat and tensing your upper body. Notice how the neck tenses and the effort is localized in your throat and your neck.

4. Notice how much effort you just used. Decrease it by half and scream "NO" again. Notice how that feels.

5. Cut the effort in half again and again scream "NO." By cutting the effort, you are reducing the tension, allowing more of your instrument to be involved in expressing anger when you say "NO."

6. Try saying "NO" from your feet, up your pelvis, and your whole body. The goal is to allow your whole body to express the anger rather than just your neck and face.

REFLECTION

■ Did you notice a difference in the amount of tension you felt as you decreased the effort each time?

■ Did the efficiency of your breath grow as you progressed through the exercise?

■ Did the sound that you produced on your "NO" feel more resonant when your breath was more efficient?

EXPLORATION: BREATH IS MOVEMENT

Imagine a glass full of water. If the glass is full, you can't pour more water into it unless you pour some out first. Like the glass of water, you can't let more air into your lungs unless you first let some out to make space for a new breath.

The vast majority of people, when asked to take a breath, will gasp for a breath. The key to breathing is to *exhale* a puff of air first, even though you might think you should inhale first. When you exhale, you create space in your lungs, allowing you to inhale effortlessly.

In this exercise, you will explore different techniques to control your breathing and voice, starting with the whispered AH. The whispered AH is one of the most basic and important procedures that Alexander encouraged his pupils to experience. It will not only enable you to use your voice properly, but it will assist you in creating a sense of calm and ease in your whole body, at rest and in action.

INHALING IS A REFLEX

As mentioned, we exhale when we speak or sing. We inhale when we get inspired. As we inhale, we infuse our body with the energy of the intention in the scene or song and our scene partners.

Acting starts when you breathe and allow another person and the situation to affect you. Your nervous system will respond naturally to your situation. If you have lines, you will say them as you exhale.

Imagine speaking like surfing the waves in the ocean. Just as the waves in the ocean provide the energy to move the surfboard, your exhale provides the energy to move your voice.

The whispered AH grew out of Alexander's very real need to find a way of using the vocal mechanism. This mechanism consists of the following components:

- **ENERGIZER:** The breath
- **VOCALIZER:** The vocal cords, where the sound originates
- **RESONATORS:** The spaces in the head and body where the sound is amplified
- **ARTICULATORS:** The lips, the teeth, and the tongue, which form and shape the sound into words

If any one of these is not working properly, it will affect the efficiency of your vocal production. For example, if you pull your head back or down, you shorten your neck muscles, which affects your vocalizer and thereby your vocal production. Similarly, if you gasp or suck in the breath, you interfere with the balance between your head and neck—this time affecting your resonators and therefore your vocal production.

In addition to the whispered AH, you'll explore the silent LA LA LA, the whispered F sound, and the whispered F to the phonated AH. This last exercise—the whispered F to the phonated AH—is an introduction to phonation, which gives voice to the sound. It is a more energized exhale.

SETUP

This exploration requires a space that is large enough for people to move around freely. If you are doing the exercise alone, you do not need much space, but if there are many people, you should be in a studio with enough room for everyone to move around without feeling constricted. If you want to sit, you will need a chair.

EXPLORATION

THE WHISPERED AH

1. From a sitting or standing position, go through Alexander's sequence of directions. To review:

   Allow your neck to be free...

   To allow your head to go forward and up...

   To allow your body to lengthen and widen...

   To allow your knees to go forward and away...

   To allow your feet to go into the ground...

   One after another, all together.

   You'll continue this sequence throughout this exercise.

2. Say "I have time."

3. Visualize, three feet in front of you, a friend, family member, or pet—someone or something that brings you joy or lightens your spirits.

   > **NOTE:** It is important that you think of someone or something real, as this will animate and engage you with your whole being, so you're not just staring into space.

4. As you go forward and up, the thought of seeing that person or thing will enliven and lift your soft palate and soften your face, creating space in the roof of your mouth and the back of your throat, effortlessly, through non-doing.

5. Direct the tip of the tongue to the top of the lower teeth. This prevents the tongue from getting in the way, shaping your mouth to form the open AH sound.

6. Let the weight of the jaw bring it forward and down. Do not tilt the head back.

7. Whisper "AHHHH...." The sound should be almost imperceptible. As you go forward and up, visualize the AH going forward and up.

8. Whispering is not a way we usually speak, so Alexander asks us to create the sound AH in an unusual way. The vowel sound AH (as in *father*) lets the air through with the least obstruction. You are not pushing to make a forced sound or a stage whisper. As you exhale, allow the vowel sound AH to lightly ride on the current of your breath.

9. After your first AH, you do not have to take a breath. Just close your lips, and the air will naturally come rushing back in through your nostrils.

10. Do several repetitions of the whispered AH, visualizing the air coming back in and giving you buoyancy and the AHs flowing out of you with ease.

REFLECTION

- After you did several whispered AHs, did you feel a change in your breathing? If so, what felt different?

- Did the length of your breath on the exhale change? How so?

- Did your level of tension decrease?

SILENT LA LA LA

1. From a sitting or standing position, go through Alexander's sequence of directions. You'll continue this sequence throughout this exercise.

2. Say "I have time."

3. Visualize, three feet in front of you, a friend, family member, or pet —someone or something that brings you joy or lightens your spirits.

4. As you allow your breath to be released, silently whisper "LA LA LA LA LA," creating the sound by fluttering your tongue up and down. Allow your jaw to stay released, without engaging it.

5. Just as with the whispered AH sound, your LA LA LAs are voiced almost silently, and do not need to be heard by anyone but yourself.

6. When you run out of breath, let the air come back in and repeat your LAs. Do not push the exhale. Tension interferes with the outward release of the breath and blocks the air from arriving in the lungs.

REFLECTION

■ After you did your LA LA LAs, did you feel a difference in the quality of your breathing?

■ Do you feel that your breath became longer and easier to sustain?

WHISPERED F SOUND

1. From a sitting or standing position, go through Alexander's sequence of directions. You'll continue this sequence throughout this exercise.

2. Say "I have time."

3. Visualize, three feet in front of you, a friend, family member, or pet—someone or something that brings you joy or lightens your spirits.

4. Allow your top teeth to rest gently behind your bottom lip and release your breath on an F sound. Make sure the jaw is loose. Do not push, squeeze or tighten on the exhalation.

5. At the end of the exhalation, allow the air to flow back into your lungs and release it on the F sound again. Notice how all the muscles coordinate to support the movement of the breath.

6. Do the process again. Think of the current that is created as the air leaves the body as a column of air that is drawing the spine upward and sustaining the energy behind the sound.

REFLECTION

- After you did your whispered Fs, did you feel a difference in the quality of your breathing? If so what was the difference?

- What did you notice regarding the air pressure behind your lips as you practiced this exercise?

THE WHISPERED F TO A PHONATED AH

1. From a sitting or standing position, go through Alexander's sequence of directions. You'll continue this sequence throughout this exercise.

2. Say "I have time."

3. Visualize, three feet in front of you, a friend, family member, or pet —someone or something that brings you joy or lightens your spirits.

4. On an exhalation, open an easy F sound to a whispered AH. As the F opens to the AH, allow it to resonate. Unlike the previous explorations, this AH is audible.

5. Explore changing the pitch as the F expands to the AH. Because you are amplifying the sound, you may feel it vibrating in your head and through your chest.

6. Switch from an F sound to an M sound followed by a whispered AH. You may feel the sound vibrating more in your facial mask (the spaces behind the bones and cartilage in your face behind your cheekbones, your nose, and just beneath your eyes, where sound resonates) and in your lips. Never force the breath, as unwanted tension pulls us off balance.

7. As you repeat, direct the sound forward and up and out toward the horizon.

REFLECTION

- As you did your phonated AHs, did you notice a difference in your breathing?

- As the sound came out, what did you notice about the tone and resonance of your voice?

REVIEW: PART I

This part covered the four tenets of the Alexander Technique—awareness, primary control, inhibition, and direction—as well as breath coordination and the voice. Consistently applying them to how you function in your daily life will allow you to move and function more efficiently. As an actor, you will be able to create a fully delineated, breathing character who may live and express any moment or action in any story. Regardless of what kind of character you are playing, or what medium, style, or period you are working in, mastering and applying these principles to your work will allow you to perform at an extraordinary level.

Alexander described his technique as one of "non-doing." When you stop doing the wrong things, the right things will start to happen on their own. One of the main benefits of practicing the Alexander Technique is that it makes you more aware of your unity and connection to yourself, the world, and the people around you (wholeness). For a character to live, actors must find wholeness within themselves.

PART II

WHOLENESS: EXPANDING AWARENESS OF THE SELF

Y ou have a sense of who you are, what your habits are, and how you move. Now you are ready to examine how you interact with, move in, and are influenced by the space in which you are working. Regardless of what character you explore or what story you tell, it all begins with yourself in the space.

As the Sufi Whirling Dervish from Turkey dances ecstatically, she clearly illustrates expansion of her body, connecting to both the earth and the heavens.

BEING IN SPACE

You have no doubt heard the phrase, "The theatre is a temple." From a historical perspective, this is literally true. The earliest theatres, dating back to 500 BC, were sacred temples and holy spaces, and the earliest forms of theatre were dances, chants, and rituals for the gods.

The Theatre at Epidaurus, Greece.
(Courtesy of Roloff Beny, Library and Archives of Canada.)

Peter Brook references this history, and the importance and power of the stage, in his book, *The Empty Space* (1968). Brook writes, "I can take any empty space and call it a bare stage. A man walks across this empty space whilst someone else is watching him, and this is all that is needed for an act of theatre to be engaged." Similarly, in creating her choreographic pieces, Twyla Tharp has stated, "I walk into a large white room…The room is lined with eight-foot-high mirrors. There's a boom box in the corner. The floor is clean, virtually spotless if you don't count the thousands of skid marks and footprints left there by dancers rehearsing. Other than the mirrors, the boom box, the skid marks, and me, the room is empty."

Whenever we begin rehearsals for a new play, we tell the actors, "Here we are. What do we have? We have ourselves. We have this play. And we have this space. What are we going to do with it? What we know is that in eight weeks, people will come in, and we will transform this space, ourselves, and the material into something amazing."

Owen Isa, offstage, about to enter the space during a production of Oklahoma. (Photo: Scott Weintraub.)

The space itself is one of your greatest tools. How you use and move in the space will inform who you are and express your story to the audience. Standing on a chair while speaking a line tells a different story and creates a totally different mood than lying down and saying the same line in the same way.

Where the story takes place will also influence how you move and behave. If your story takes place outside, there are questions you need to ask and explore. For example:

- What are the natural elements in the space in which the story takes place?

- Is it raining?

- Is there a storm?

- Are you in the desert?

- Are you walking through a forest? If so, are the trees in ordered rows? Are there branches blowing wildly and obstructing your path?

Your relationship to nature and to the elements can be a powerful influence and tool in terms of how you move in and create the specific reality of the space. This skill of being in space with natural conditions and elements is vital, whether you are working on a theatrical stage, on a sound stage, or before a green screen.

> **NOTE:** Just as being in the space changes you, your presence in the space changes it.

Much of Jez Butterworth's play *Jerusalem* takes place in front of a beat-up trailer in a forest in England. The first five minutes of the play consist of the protagonist, Johnny "Rooster" Byron, entering and performing his morning ritual. Mark Rylance created the role at the Royal Court Theatre in London and also performed it on Broadway. His performance was a master class in informing character and space without speaking a word. As Byron, Rylance walked in front of the trailer, made his breakfast, washed up in a tub of water, stretched, belched, and so on. By the end of these first five minutes, without having heard a line of dialogue, the audience not only knew exactly who Byron was, but also that this little space was his territory.

Fully understanding your relationship to space, and how you use space, will give you the command and freedom to create specific moments. With this practical understanding, you will be able to create and connect your whole being to the depth, distance, and vista of the space as soon as you enter it. Moreover, the scale of the space will automatically enable you to adjust physically and vocally to open, fill, and broaden your communication, and thus include the audience in its entirety. Even if you are working in front of a camera, where there is a level of intimacy and closeness quite different from working on a large stage, an acute awareness of the space you are in will help you create the environment in which you will be acting.

To Ridley Scott, the space in which a scene takes place is much more than just space. In a 2013 interview published in the *New York Times Magazine*, Scott notes, "Universe to me is, if you'd like, the final character. Your landscape in a western is one of the most important characters the film has. The best westerns are about man against his own landscape."

WATCH THIS MOVIE: *GRAVITY* (2013)

In the film *Gravity*, not only did the location of the characters in space affect their behavior, movement patterns, and psychological tension, but space was also the story's primary antagonist—to the point where the main character, played by Sandra Bullock, says, "I hate space."

Despite the brilliance of the technology and the filmmakers' ability to create the feeling of weightlessness through CGI, it was the actors' ability to express the vastness of space that made it feel real to the audience. In many scenes, Bullock hung from wires before a green screen. As an actor, Bullock's challenge was to avoid being trapped by the technical devices carrying and controlling her. Although she was bound by gravity, she had to create the illusion she was floating in a void.

Many shots in the movie were tight close-ups, meaning that the only tool Bullock had to convey what she was seeing was her gaze. How she achieved this is explained in the following excerpts from an interview we conducted with the film's choreographer, Francesca Jaynes:

"It's so interesting working with Sandra Bullock. She's highly intelligent, highly intuitive. When I was first brought on, it was a fascinating job, because no one really knew what their job was going to be. It was all so new.

"Nikki Penny, the visual effects producer, rang me up and said, 'I don't know if there's a job for you, but would you please come meet Sandra and [director] Alfonso Cuarón? This is such a technical project for Sandra. She's going to be very alone, and I'm afraid no one's going to be looking at the beauty of the movement.'

"So, I went and met with Alfonso, and fell in love with him, because he's so passionate about movement in space and it being poetry. Then I met Sandra. I told her about all these exercises that might help her with the weightlessness. But she's not that kind of actor. She didn't want to do them at all. So, we watched footage of astronauts and the International Space Station, and she loved it. She just got it. She was actually able to look at the rhythm and just copy it.

"If, for instance, Sandra had to pick something up and unscrew it, I would work it out as rhythm—as a count. And we would practice it as a count until Sandra had it in her body. Then she would do it without the count, because having me count out loud interfered with her ability to act. We worked through things in tiny segments, with a count and a rhythm.

Sandra Bullock as Ryan Stone in Gravity. *Francesca Jaynes assisted her in floating in zero gravity in a virtual environment.*

"A lot of people thought it was all animated. Well, of course, there's a lot of animation, but to animate it, we had to get the position of the body and the head right, and the dynamic had to be right for the narrative. So, we worked with puppeteers and stunt people.

"Sometimes, it was just by instinct. When you're in zero gravity, every action has an opposite and equal reaction. So, if I'm to touch you, I move back afterward with the same amount of force. We didn't have a technical device to make sure we did it accurately, so Sandra had to trust herself and Alfonso."

You can read more about Jaynes's work in Appendix C.

EXPLORATION: GAZING AT THE HORIZON

When you first walk into any space, the most important thing you can do is help the audience visualize what you see in front of you. Whether you are trying to create the illusion that you have walked into a canyon, a restaurant, or someone's attic, you must relate to the environment you are in on a physical and emotional level. Achieving this often involves gazing at and relating to what you see on the horizon. What you see on the horizon informs both your character and the character of the space.

Gazing at the horizon involves your whole body,
from the top of your head to the bottom of your feet.

The goal of this exploration is for you to find a connection to your body in different kinds of space—both intimate and public—that are familiar to all of us. You'll do this by imagining you are gazing into the horizon. Once you have decided what you are seeing on the horizon, you will be able to move in the space with a specific awareness of where you are and what you see around you.

Gazing at the horizon. (Photo: Todd Domenic Cribari.)

SETUP

You can do this exploration alone or in a group. If doing this exploration in a group, a group leader should coach the group with the instructions. It is preferable to work in a large, open space so you have distance and perspective within the environment.

EXPLORATION

1. Place your feet hip-width apart. Make sure your big toe, first toe, and second toe are pointing forward, and that your feet are parallel. (A turned-out posture tightens the hips and lower back, preventing the neck from being free.) Allow yourself to breathe fully.

2. Tell yourself, "I have time."

3. Picture yourself standing at your favorite beach, mountain, or desert, and look straight ahead. Imagine you are looking at the farthest horizon, where the sky would meet the land or sea.

4. Letting your gaze guide you, slowly turn 360 degrees, looking at the horizon all around you, at the exact point where the land or sea ends and the sky begins.

5. Extend your whole arm, lengthening from your shoulder to your fingers, toward the horizon. Notice that your head is much higher on your spine, and that your whole body feels taller.

6. Gently pivot your head slightly up and down to allow your neck muscles to release.

7. Leading up with your head, and keeping your eyes on the horizon, walk around in the space. Allow your steps to be deliberate. Continue to look at the horizon as you walk. Be curious and investigate the space. Walk as if you were discovering details in the environment—say, a shell, a tree branch, or a stone on the ground. Be aware of the many sensations in the environment—the smells and sounds, and maybe even the feel of a breeze or the heat of the sun on your skin.

8. If you are working in a group, relate to the people around you. Recognize them as they recognize you. Alternatively, relate to people in your imagination. Spot them approaching you from the horizon —an old friend, a deceased relative you never made peace with, or a jilted lover. Greet them, shake their hands, touch them. Continue to be aware of the horizon within the context of these interactions.

9. Walk toward the center of the space. Stop and look out toward the horizon. If you are performing this exercise with others, share this moment of being engaged with the space and each other in a common activity.

REFLECTION

- When you were gazing at the horizon, did you feel you were taller? As you tried to see the farthest distance did it elevate you more? Did you feel more expansive and freer in your whole body, both when still and when walking?

- Was your imagination stimulated by having so much space around you?

- Did the image of the horizon you created influence how you moved and felt? How?

WATCH THIS MOVIE: *LAWRENCE OF ARABIA* (1962)

In the film *Lawrence of Arabia* (1962), Peter O'Toole as T. E. Lawrence gazes at the horizon, looking at the unknown, threatening figure approaching —a perfect example of looking at the horizon. Director David Lean is incredibly aware of the relationship between the human figure and the scope and scale of the space. Throughout the entire film, there are countless moments and sequences that depict the characters dealing with the sheer amplitude of their environment.

Peter O'Toole as T. E. Lawrence in the film Lawrence of Arabia, *gazing at the horizon.* (Columbia Pictures.)

EXPLORATION: CREATING A COMMON HORIZON

This exploration is crucial when you are collaborating with other actors. It ensures that all people in the scene are inhabiting and experiencing the same environment. Understanding what you are seeing on the horizon is important, whether you are outside (beach, forest, or mountain) or inside (restaurant, conference room, or prison).

> **NOTE:** Creating a common environment with a scene partner will help you, no matter what the environment of the scene.

SETUP

Do this exercise with a scene partner. You will work together to discover what you see on the horizon, taking turns adding elements to the view and embellishing them.

EXPLORATION

1. Decide with your scene partner what kind of environment you are seeing—a forest, a meadow, the ocean, an urban skyline, or something else.

2. Enter the space and look at the horizon. Let what you see affect how you stand, breathe, and feel.

3. Your scene partner enters the space, stands next to you, and asks, "What do you see?"

4. Tell your scene partner what you see—for example, "I see the ocean."

5. Your scene partner answers, "I see it, too." He or she then adds another element, pointing to exactly where it is and articulating what it is—for example, saying, "Look, over there I see a boat."

6. Agree with your partner and then define the specific qualities of the boat. For example, say, "I see it, too; it's a sailboat with red sails."

7. Keep going back and forth with your partner, adding and embellishing specific details to each new scenic element until you both feel you have a clear picture. Then move on to the other elements you see.

By the end of the exercise, as you and your partner gaze at the horizon, you should both have a shared vision of exactly what you see. In our ocean example, you would know the type of boat, the color of the sky, the placement of the sun, where the clouds are, what kind they are, the time of day, the state of the tide, the choppiness of the water, whether there are people playing in the ocean, whether there is any sea life, the nature of the coastline, and so on.

8. If you are working on a scene, enter again, and start the scene as if you were in the environment you just created.

REFLECTION

- Were you able to create a common environment with your partner?

- When you conveyed what appeared on the horizon, did it help you feel like you were both inhabiting the same space?

- If you had a scene to work on, did having this shared environment inform the beginning of the scene?

- Once you started this scene, did the fact you had a common environment feed the scene in some way? How?

EXPLORATION: DILATION OF THE BODY IN SPACE (KINESPHERE)

Dominance in human behavior is demonstrated physically by a higher relationship of the head to the spine. People who are confident and powerful and dominant move in an expansive way, often making themselves physically bigger, to demonstrate their power.

The idea that making yourself physically bigger makes you appear more powerful originates with animals. The elk with the largest antlers, the lion with the most impressive mane, and the bull elephant with the longest tusks are the most fearsome and powerful animals in their respective groups. They are followed because they are the alpha males, the leaders of the pack. The other animals bow before them, demonstrating that they are lower in the hierarchy, and so it is with humans.

Many animals are able to make themselves appear bigger to establish dominance. (Courtesy of Matt Gibson, Getty Images.)

What do kings and queens wear? Crowns. And the pope? A mitre. Indian chiefs wear headdresses. Why? Because this headgear creates height, a symbolic connection between the wearers and a higher power, and the sense that they are bigger, more dominant, and higher in status than those around them.

The actual spaces that powerful people function in reinforce this construction of power. A king rules from an elevated throne. A priest preaches from a pulpit. A CEO often has an office on the highest floor of a skyscraper and sits behind a large desk. Indeed, in their quest to assert power over a group, humans use whatever tools they can. This creates spatial distance between themselves and those they perceive to be beneath them. And athletes frequently raise their arms in triumph, unconsciously making themselves larger and more intimidating.

Bo Eason, formerly of the Houston Oilers, elevates and lengthens in victory. (Courtesy of Bo Eason.)

WATCH THESE MOVIES: *ELIZABETH I* (2005), *THE QUEEN* (2006), AND *THE AUDIENCE* (2013)

Throughout her long and varied career, Helen Mirren has played many monarchs in both theatre and film, including Queen Elizabeth I in *Elizabeth I* (2005) and Queen Elizabeth II in *The Queen* (2006) and in both the stage and film versions of *The Audience* (2013). She is the master of using the relationship between her head and her whole body to connect to and convey the power and dominance of these monarchs, regardless of the time period or nationality.

In this exploration, you'll examine dilation (expansion). This exercise is designed to give you the means to move effectively and powerfully in space and to enable you to literally expand, both psychologically and physically. This process will also help you communicate your intentions much more clearly and facilitate ease, power, and support in your vocal delivery.

This time-lapse photo demonstrates how the body expands as it moves through space. (Courtesy of Robert Witkowski.)

SETUP

For this exercise, it is preferable to work in a large open space. If working in a group, stand in a circle. Before the exercise, repeat two or three times, "I have time."

EXPLORATION

1. Place your feet parallel to each other, hip-width apart. Feel the weight of your body on your feet, distributed evenly from your heels to the balls of your feet.

2. Notice if you are tightening your ankles. If you are, loosen them by gently shifting your weight forward onto the balls of your feet and then back on your heels. Do this a few times until you find the center between the balls of your feet and your heels. Be sure to soften behind your knees.

3. Gaze out at the farthest horizon and gently pivot your head up and down on top of your first vertebra (the atlas) to ensure that your neck and head move freely.

4. Imagine you have a searchlight that emits light from the crown of your head. Turn it on so that the searchlight shines 100 feet up into the air.

5. As you shine the searchlight upward, imagine your feet are growing roots 100 feet into the ground. These roots don't anchor or tether you to the soil; rather, they serve as a foundation—a source of energy and support—as they penetrate deep into the earth. Notice how this feels.

6. Imagine you have the ability to release the roots growing down, enabling you to walk through the space. Before each footstep, release the roots that have grown into the ground; then, as you complete each step, grow new ones through the foot. Continue to imagine the searchlight beaming from the top of your head and the roots growing deeper and deeper into the ground as you move.

7. Return to stillness or, if working in a group, return to the circle.

8. Allow your arms to hang gently by your sides and imagine that each of your fingers is a tiny flashlight.

9. Turn on every flashlight. Allow a beam of light to emit from each finger and shine onto the floor.

10. Allow your finger-lights to slowly lift your arms up in front of you, open them to either side, and raise them above your head.

11. Continue to imagine the searchlight beaming from the top of your head and the roots growing from the bottom of your feet, and let your finger-lights guide your arms to move freely. Shine your lights on all the surfaces of the space.

As the searchlight beams upward from the crown of your head and the finger lights shine outward from your hands, the roots from your feet extend deep into the earth.

12. Move and expand through the space, remaining aware of the farthest horizon. Notice how this feels.

13. Stop moving or return to the circle and allow your arms to come to rest at your sides.

14. Imagine that all of your skin and clothing is porous and translucent, like rice paper. Now imagine there is a light in the center of your body and turn it on. It is a golden, bright source of light, and its rays shine through the pores of your skin in every direction.

15. Feel the light coming out of the center of your body, forward, sideways, and backward, illuminating every wall of the space. This light is not just a glow inside you; it is a bright, all-encompassing light, emanating from the core of your being, expanding you in the space. The rays of your light fill the space in every direction. Breathe through every pore and ray of light, allowing the breath to fuel your entire being, and sense your energy expanding into space.

The bright, all-encompassing light, emanating from the core of your being, expanding you in the space.

16. While maintaining this awareness and all these visualizations—the searchlight from your head, the roots from your feet, the flashlights from your fingers, and the lantern at the center of your body shining outward—begin moving throughout the space once again.

> **TIP:** If you are in a group, become as aware of the others' lights as you are of your own. Also, keep making random and dynamic changes in direction so that everyone is moving in different directions.

17. When you feel you have explored the space to your satisfaction for some time, return to stillness or, if working in a group, to the circle.

REFLECTION

- What did you feel?

- What did you notice?

- Did the idea of the light help you expand?

- Did the different lights emanating from you—the searchlight from the top, the light from your fingertips, the light from within your center—influence, in different ways, how you moved and felt?

- Were you able to differentiate between the different qualities of these lights?

- Were you able to use the power of the roots in conjunction with the light?

- Did it unify your movement or did you feel that the light and the roots were at odds with each other?

- Did you feel more connected to the other actors?

- Were you able to balance the sense of light and fluidity with the sense of weight and power?

- Did it help you to visualize all these elements at once, and did you get a sense of all the directions happening simultaneously?

RELATING TO OBJECTS

Ever since humans developed opposable thumbs and could pick things up, objects have been an integral part of our existence. It makes sense, then, that every object in a scene can be a useful tool to inform character and story.

The objects around you reflect your stature, power, taste, style, beliefs, and education. If you are royalty, these objects will likely be expensive, be handcrafted, and have historical and symbolic significance. If you are a sergeant in the army, your quarters, though spartan, will include the things most important to you—your weapons, a photograph of a loved one, a pinup calendar, or perhaps a favorite libation. If you are a struggling, Depression-era housewife, your household furnishings might be old, rickety, and threadbare.

The kinds of objects and furnishings a character surrounds themselves with, and how they use them, don't just reveal who the character is; they might be the key to the character or even the entire story.

When depicting a character, you could make a stereotypical selection about what that character drinks from: for example, the king, a silver chalice; the sergeant, a tin cup; the housewife, a cracked glass. Alternatively, you can make a more significant and specific choice that adds a new element to the character. The sergeant's tin cup could be one he's had for years that serves as a talisman of sorts, or he could drink from a flask left to him by a comrade killed in battle. The housewife's glass, though cracked, could be a family heirloom—the last one of a set of crystal glasses that reminds her of better days past. And although the king might lounge about on a brocade-covered chaise and the housewife on a worn-out, lumpy couch, both might find comfort and warmth from these objects because of their familiar look, smell, and feel.

We can learn so much about an object through the sense of touch.
(Photo: Todd Domenic Cribari.)

Just as you must put thought and care into how you use your body and enter a space, you must do so with respect to how you handle objects and your relationship to them. Something as simple as picking up a piece of paper and reading it can move a plot forward and inform character. There are major plot points in plays and films that revolve around a character reading a document—a love letter, a legal document, a map, or a will. What the document means to you will influence how you handle and read it.

As you enter a space, you notice the objects gradually. There is an organic progression of discovery when you first explore an environment. First, there's the furniture and the layout of the room: the table is here, the chairs are here, and the door is there. Then there's how you respond to these objects. For example, when you are about to eat dinner in someone's home, there is a difference between simply sitting down at the table without taking notice of the chairs and commenting on how nice the chairs are before you sit down. It says something about you—that you noticed the owner has nice chairs as well as the taste and resources to acquire them. Moreover, how you sit down in a nice chair will be different from how you sit down in, say, a drab metal folding chair.

When we talk about objects and how you handle and relate to them, we are referring to the memories you associate with an object and to your connection to the history of the object and its origin. Even if you are not handling an object yourself, you still need to understand your relationship to it. The cavalier and offhand attitude with which most of us deal with objects today does not serve us well in creating a reason for, and a connection to, the objects we use (or avoid) in a scene and in the environment. The explorations that follow will help you endow the objects you handle with emotional weight and history.

WATCH THESE MOVIES:
DANGEROUS LIAISONS (1988)
AND *NEBRASKA* (2013)

In the movie *Dangerous Liaisons*, John Malkovich, as the Vicomte de Valmont, is engaged in a contest of wills with the Marquise de Merteuil (Glenn Close), having bet that he can seduce and manipulate the chaste Madame de Tourvel (Michelle Pfeiffer) and virginal Cécile de Volanges (Uma Thurman). Throughout the story, love letters delivered by Valmont and others are the vehicle through which this deceit is carried out.

The back and forth of the letters is almost like the back and forth of a particularly vicious tennis match. In every scene in which Malkovich handles a letter, he varies the way he handles it, conveying both the import of each letter's contents and the way he is affected by it. In one scene he drops it with great disdain into Thurman's lap. In another, he casually twirls it in his fingers. One time, he reveals it just for a second, so the recipient can see that he is in possession of the letter and thereby in control of the situation. Another time, he presents it with great ceremony, as if it were a treasure. He never simply delivers the letter.

In a film that is, at its root, entirely about control and power, the weight and import of these letters is conveyed cleverly and specifically by how all the actors in the film handle the object.

John Malkovich, as the Vicomte de Valmont, mischievously delivers a letter in Dangerous Liaisons.

This is in direct contrast to the letter in *Nebraska* (2013) that notifies Bruce Dern's character, Woody Grant, that he has won a million dollars. Although everyone else realizes it is a scam, to him, this letter is endowed with the power to change his life. So, he takes great care of it, handling it as if it were a "golden ticket" from *Willy Wonka & the Chocolate Factory*.

Bruce Dern as Woody Grant handles his award notification letter with great care throughout Nebraska.
(Paramount Pictures.)

EXPLORATION: EXPERIENCING AN OBJECT THROUGH THE SENSES

The way we usually identify objects is by looking at them. When we use only our sense of sight to experience an object, however, we limit how much we can learn about it.

Experiencing our world through our whole bodies and all of our senses creates a more integrated connection to ourselves and the objects we use. There is something profound about feeling the weight of a stone, the smoothness of a leaf, or the smell of a flower. The infinite variation of the senses is what makes our world colorful and expansive, yet personal.

The following exercise will help you explore your relationship to an object using all your senses. The purpose of this exercise is to use all your senses to observe the details of an object and how objects affect our emotional, physical, and psychological state.

SETUP

Two people should perform this exploration. One person will be blindfolded, while the other will hand them different objects. Then, these roles will be reversed.

Before the exercise begins, each person should choose five objects, different in some or all of the following qualities:

- Weight
- Size
- Shape
- Density
- Texture
- Smell
- Taste
- Temperature
- Sound

These could include everyday objects such as a flower or piece of food, or something more interesting, like a bowl of water, a piece of fur, a silk scarf, an ice cube, a lipstick, or a squishy toy—anything that might surprise the senses. Make sure each person is unaware of which objects the other has chosen, perhaps placing them in separate boxes or bags.

When you are blindfolded, your objective will be to learn as much as you can about each object using all your other available senses. This exercise should take between 15 and 20 minutes per person.

EXPLORATION

NOTE: This exploration assumes that you will start as the person who is blindfolded.

1. Put on a blindfold and sit on the floor. Be aware of your head-to-spine relationship. Allow yourself to lengthen away from your sits bones. Stay relaxed and alert.

2. Say to yourself, "I have time," and allow yourself to exhale. Let out a few sighs.

3. Open your palm to accept the first object from your partner.

4. After your partner places the object in your hand, hold it. Allow its weight to interact with your hand and with gravity. Take your time to experience the weight and shape of the object.

5. Explore different aspects of the object as thoroughly as possible. For example, use the object to massage your body, toss it from hand to hand, taste it, smell it, rest upon it, or use it to make sounds. Touch it both firmly and gently to detect details or irregularities of the surface of the object.

6. As you explore the object through your senses, allow yourself to respond emotionally to the object. Notice any visual images that arise in your mind from your interaction with the object. Breathe and take your time. Feel free to respond with sound.

7. Ponder the following questions:
   - What is the object made of?
   - What is the object used for?
   - Is it a special, one-of-a-kind, handmade object, or is it a mass-produced, common one?

- Is the object man-made or is it from nature?

- Is the object new or old?

- What color do you think the object is?

8. When you have finished exploring the object, put it down and open your palm for the next one.

9. Repeat the preceding steps, taking your time and using all your senses to fully experience the new object.

10. After you have explored all five objects, take off your blindfold and examine each of the objects you handled.

11. Switch places with your partner and repeat the exercise, handing them your objects.

REFLECTION

■ Were there some objects you were more comfortable with or that you related to on a personal level?

■ Did any objects surprise you? How? Why?

■ Did any objects change your mood? Why?

■ Once you saw an object, did it look the way you thought it would?

WATCH THIS MOVIE:
PERFUME: THE STORY OF A MURDERER (2006)

In the film *Perfume* (2006), Ben Whishaw plays a serial murderer who, after murdering his female victims, distills their remains into the perfect scent. Notice the care and focus with which Whishaw handles the chemicals, vials, and ingredients of his scents, and especially how he engages his entire being in the act of smelling and savoring his concoctions.

EXPLORATION: OBJECT AWARENESS DETECTIVE

This is a companion exploration to the last one. Whereas the focus of the previous exploration was learning about and creating a relationship with objects without a sense of sight, this one deals with observation through both sight and your other senses.

Understanding the importance and emotional value of the objects around you or that you handle in a scene is a valuable skill in your work as an actor. As the rhythm of our lives accelerates and our everyday existence becomes more complicated, it is easy to lose the ability to be honest and present with the objects in our lives. We cannot stress enough the importance of creating specific, authentic connections to the objects, props, and furniture in a scene.

> **NOTE:** Later we will explore in more depth how you can create a deep bond to the moment, to objects, and to others.

SETUP

This exploration is meant to be performed by a group. One person will assume the role of curator and will gather at least 20 disparate objects. These might include toys, business cards, photographs, tools, masks, a music box, a snow globe, and so on. With the other participants outside the room, the curator should arrange the objects on a large table and cover them with a cloth so they cannot be seen. The other participants will be divided into groups of two or three. Each group will need paper and a pen.

> **NOTE:** The greater the variety and range of the object's type, age, and function, the better.

A variety of random objects ready for discovery!
(Photo: Todd Domenic Cribari.)

EXPLORATION

NOTE: This exploration assumes you are one of the participants rather than the curator.

1. Gather around the table with your group and the other participants, and watch as the curator removes the cloth to reveal the objects.

2. For the next 10 minutes, silently observe and handle the objects, learning as much about each object as you can. Your goal is to determine what each object is, where it is from, and what its condition is. Rotate around the table so you can observe and interact with all the objects. At the end of 10 minutes, the curator re-covers the objects with the cloth.

3. Sit with your group and write down as many details as you remember about as many objects as you can. When you are finished, gather together with the other participants and the curator.

4. Together with your group, name one of the objects and describe all the details you can recall.

5. The curator will ask if any other groups noted other details about the object in question until no one else has anything more to add. The curator will then reveal the object.

6. The next group should name another object and the details they recall, and ask other groups to note additional details. Repeat this process until no objects remain.

REFLECTION

- Working in groups, could you recall every object?

- Which details, and how many of them, could you remember?

- Did everyone use all their senses and powers of observation to explore each object thoroughly?

- Were you limited by the time?

- Did some participants tend to remember tactile things—texture, material, and composition—while others recalled details of workmanship, writing, and labels?

- Did some participants explore the objects more thoroughly—shaking them or trying to turn them on if there was a mechanism?

- Were there certain details or objects that the entire group failed to remember?

RELATING TO OTHERS

Perhaps you have noticed that so far, we have asked you to interact primarily with objects and your environment rather than with other human beings. This is because connecting and relating to another person in an authentic and compelling way is impossible if you haven't done all this other work first.

To believe that you can just walk into a scene and start relating to someone is not just putting the cart before the horse; it's akin to a soldier charging into battle without first learning to wield their weapon or a doctor entering an operating room surgery without knowing the patient, diagnosis, or what tools they need to perform the operation.

Connecting to your body, relating to your environment and the space, and interacting with the objects around you in a functional way is the fundamental process you must undergo before you can connect to another person. The Alexander Technique will enable you to bring all these elements together as an integrated whole.

Relating to each other in silence. (Photo: Todd Domenic Cribari.)

At its heart, acting is all about relationship, communication, and connection with other people. The following explorations will guide you through the most effective way of working with others—first in silence while focusing on the physical aspects of an interaction with another person in the space and in the story, and then through the layering of intent, sound, and text.

What you will experience in these explorations—being present, open, and engaged with another human being—is fundamental to creating honest, authentic work as an actor. The heart of every scene, regardless of the genre, is people relating to each other. These explorations will help you connect your inner world to the outer world and to the people with whom you are relating.

The explorations in this part will help you to discover and connect anew with your true impulses. Trust your director, the material, and, above all else, the people with whom you are working.

BEWARE OF PRE-SHAPING

Particularly when doing a play you are familiar with, there is a danger of pre-shaping a scene. *Pre-shaping* a scene is when you plan out what you will do and feel before you even start. This is similar to *end-gaining*—feeling like we need to figure out what's happening in a given circumstance before we discover and experience it. Pre-shaping often results in stereotypical and contrived choices and ultimately serves neither the character nor the play.

EXPLORATION: WORKING IN SILENCE (MUTUAL GAZE)

So often in our daily lives, and especially in our scene work with other actors, we approach our work with a predetermined agenda. This does not serve us well and leads to end-gaining. Your goal, as an actor and as a human being, is to be present with the people who you are working with and to be open to receiving their energy and sharing your own with them.

This exploration distills this skill to its most elemental form. You will start with a line from a play or a film in your mind, but the objective is not to communicate this line; it is simply to use it as a starting point for an exchange with another actor.

SETUP

You can do this simple exercise, which takes 20 minutes, in a group or with a partner. It should be done in a room that is absolutely quiet, with a door that can be locked from the inside so no one can interfere with the experience.

Have enough chairs on hand for everyone. A leader should guide the process. If working in a group, pair up with a partner—preferably someone you do not know well. It is often helpful to work with someone with whom you are unfamiliar.

EXPLORATION

1. Find a space in the room and sit on a chair, facing your partner from about two feet away. Look into your partner's eyes and maintain eye contact.

2. Position your sits bones toward the front of the chair so your back does not touch the chair. Place both feet flat on the floor. Lengthen, widen, and tell yourself, "I have time."

3. Choose a short line from a play, song, or poem and mentally repeat it. Communicate this line to your partner only through your eyes and your body. Your partner should do the same. Neither of you should speak or attempt to "act out," indicate, or convey your line physically; this exercise is about nonverbal communication and exchange between you and your partner.

> **NOTE:** The line you are thinking of is merely the starting point. It usually transforms into something else or disappears from your mind as you become more involved in the interaction with your partner.

4. Be open and receptive to your partner's communication and energy, and be willing to respond. As emotions come up, feel free to laugh, cry, and express yourself with sound—but do so without speaking. It is common to experience a wide range of contrasting emotions during this exercise!

5. After 15 minutes, the leader will ask participants to express gratitude to their partner for their gift of attention. The leader should then ask everyone to sit in a circle and share their experiences.

REFLECTION

- How did you feel? Frustrated? At peace?

- Did you feel like you were receiving energy and emotion from your partner?

- Did you reflect the energy and emotion you received back, or did you change it to something else?

- After a while, did you achieve a level of comfort with your partner?

- Did you feel you were better at receiving information from your partner or giving it?

  Some people feel they can do both. Others feel that while they initially focus on transmitting their line, they begin to find what they are receiving from their partner more interesting—to the point that they stop thinking about their line and become fully engaged in the interaction. The essence of the moment becomes more important than what is happening in their own heads.

- As the exercise progressed, did you feel more of an emotional connection to your partner?

- Did you find it difficult to open yourself up to your partner and freely exchange emotions through your eyes, opting instead to try to only stare at your partner and avoid the vulnerability encouraged in this exercise?

  Just as we worked to identify physical habits earlier on, this may be evidence of an interpersonal habit you should be aware of and work on going forward.

EXPLORATION: BUS STOP

In the previous exploration, everything you did came from yourself and your partner. Although you started with a line in your head, that was just the jumping-off point. Where you went with it and how the experience progressed stemmed from your ability to exchange energy and emotion with your partner. In this exploration, you will do the same thing, but this time you will introduce fundamental script elements—a setting, a basic objective, and a character driven by an emotion or condition.

You will perform this exercise, which involves an improvised scene at a bus stop, with a partner. For this exercise, you will create a character based on one strong emotion—for example, anger, fear, jealousy, confusion, nervousness, joy, delight, or excitement—and your partner will create a character based on a contrasting emotion. Your character will be the essence and embodiment of your chosen emotion; throughout the exercise, every choice you make, and everything you say and do, should be driven by this one emotion.

Two actors relating to each other in a different situation and setting.
(Photo: Todd Domenic Cribari.)

This exploration is most effective if the actors are not aware of their partner's chosen emotion beforehand. If you and your partner are part of a larger group, and there is a group leader, that person should speak privately with you and your partner to ensure you have not chosen the same emotion. If there is no leader, and you and your partner realize you have chosen the same emotion as the scene unfolds, one of you should move toward a different emotion.

In addition to choosing an emotion, you and your partner should decide where the bus you are waiting for is taking you, why you are going there, and how you feel about it—but again, do not share any of these choices with each other.

> **NOTE:** This exercise can be especially effective when you are rehearsing a play to see how the play's characters would relate to each other in a different setting.

SETUP

Place a bench or two chairs side by side in the center of the room to represent the bus stop.

EXPLORATION

1. Imagine you and your partner are waiting for a bus. As you wait, improvise a scene in which you communicate the emotion you have chosen in how you move, stand, speak, and react to each other.

2. See where the scene goes, filtering each choice you make through your chosen emotions. The scene should last between three and five minutes.

REFLECTION

■ Although you were focused on playing the essence of the emotion, did you find you could create a believable, realistic person?

■ Did the single-mindedness of the other character enhance your character's choices?

■ Did you find yourself picking up on the other character's emotion, or were you able to stay with your own?

■ Did you find yourself building other character qualities on top of the emotion during the scene—for example, age, occupation, or history?

EXPLORATION: THE AUTHENTIC MOVEMENT

Using her knowledge of dance and Jungian psychoanalysis, dance therapist Mary Starks Whitehouse designed a remarkable educational method in the 1950s to integrate mind, body, and emotion. This method, called *Authentic Movement,* is an effective way for actors to enhance their awareness of their physical, emotional, and psychological interferences (blocks) and to open and connect their emotional selves through movement.

Authentic Movement derives its name from the fact that the movement stems from an internal impulse that arises from what is happening in the moment. It is unnecessary to move until you actually feel an *impulse* to move. This experience is extremely effective in connecting ourselves with the truth in our bodies—that intangible, yet very real, energy and force that honestly reflects what we are feeling.

This exploration is a perfect way to connect with another actor during rehearsals of a scene that is not working, feels disjointed, or has become an automatic repetition of line readings. Often, the major source of interference is a lack of relationship and truth. Using the Authentic Movement method, actors will be able to connect to the body, the moment, and each other, and serve the scene. The body never lies.

SETUP

You will perform this exercise with a partner. If possible, pair up with an actor you have not worked with previously or with whom you are less familiar. If you and your partner are part of a larger group, choose a leader to spearhead the process. (The steps here assume there is a leader.)

One actor in each pair will be the "mover," who moves about during the exercise; the other, the "witness," who monitors the mover's movement and guides them when necessary.

The mover's eyes should remain closed throughout the exercise. The witness will stand and move near the mover, but should intervene only if the mover is in danger of colliding with something or someone else.

Otherwise, the witness should not interfere with the experience of the mover. The witness must remain mindful and focused to guide the mover in such a way as to guarantee their freedom and their safety without being overprotective.

There should be no talking between the mover and the witness. The witness should only follow the mover and provide a gentle touch to guide the mover in a safe direction, as needed.

> **CAUTION:** If you are working in a group, this exercise may become quite chaotic. If the studio you are working in does not provide ample space for physical exploration and freedom of movement, divide the group into fewer pairs and have them take turns performing the exercise.

EXPLORATION

> **NOTE:** This exploration assumes you will start as the mover.

1. Find an open space. You can begin by lying down, sitting, or standing, with the witness close by, but far enough away to avoid interfering. Close your eyes and keep them closed for the duration of the exercise.

2. When you sense an impulse, allow yourself to move with it without judgment or control.

   You might repeat the movement rhythmically—first as a small movement and then allowing it to grow in shape or intensity. This movement might catapult you into space, without your knowing where you're going to land. Or it might cause you to be upright with your arms suspended. The experience of moving from an impulse might help you morph into a different shape, an animal, or an inanimate object. It might be completely void of reason and connection, or it might tell a story in which you find yourself lost. Just keep trusting your impulses and keep moving.

3. After 20 minutes, the leader will ask the movers to slow down to a stop. Keep your eyes closed and breathe deeply. Notice how you feel.

4. The leader will ask the movers to open their eyes slowly.

5. Move to a corner of the studio with your witness to briefly discuss what you noticed, felt, and experienced during the exploration.

6. Switch roles and repeat the exercise.

7. At the end of the exercise, gather with the whole group in a circle. The leader will invite participants to discuss their experiences and what they found valuable.

> **TIP:** Allow each person to speak. If there is not enough time for everyone to share their feelings, something is lost in the exercise as a whole. Make sure you leave enough time for this final stage.

Authentic movement: While the "movers" blindly explore their impulses as they move through space, the "witnesses" observe and ensure their safety.
(Photo: Todd Domenic Cribari.)

REFLECTION

- How did you feel?

- Was your imagination sparked by this experience?

- Were you able to trust your physical impulses?

- Did anything interfere with the process? If so, what? Were you able to overcome this distraction and allow your body to move freely?

- Did you become more comfortable during the course of the exploration? If so, did the quality of your movement change as you became more comfortable?

- Was it easier for you to be the mover or the witness?

- As the mover, did you feel the presence of your witness?

- As the witness, how did you feel about having the responsibility of keeping the mover safe?

- As the witness, did you find yourself moving in a similar rhythm and style as your mover? If so, did you notice and embrace that impulse?

This will often happen as the mirror neurons (the neurons that activate when we are both in action and observing an action) are firing without your consciousness or any impulse on your part. This is a physiological event that you may have noticed when watching a boxing match or an action-packed scene in a movie. If you are in sync with your partner, there will be a physical and emotional symbiosis between the two of you. This emotional and physical give and take is what we are hoping will happen in this exploration, and what we all are aiming for when we are acting with a scene partner.

WATCH THIS MOVIE: *ROOM* (2015)

Although we see examples of authentic movement in many films and plays, a film that best exemplifies what authentic movement looks and feels like is Lenny Abrahamson's 2015 film *Room*.

In the story, the two protagonists, Ma (Academy Award winner Brie Larson) and her son Jack (Jacob Tremblay), are imprisoned in a tiny shed. So, they are forced to work together physically and emotionally, both as mover and witness, in virtually every moment of every day of their lives.

Because Ma wants to create as normal a life as she can for her son, she has attempted to build a routine in their lives where they can do the things regular people do—play, exercise, imagine, walk, clean, cook, and eat. As you watch this film, notice how the two of them are in sync in all these activities, both physically and emotionally. Despite the tiny space that they inhabit, they find ways to move, feel joy, and create a human experience together.

Brie Larson as Ma and Jacob Tremblay as her son, Jack, move in tandem, always aware of each other, applying the principle of authentic movement, in Room. (A24.)

ENTERING THE WORLD OF THE STORY

When we relate to each other, we must also relate to the objects, activities, natural world, and everything else that surrounds us. It is then, when we are fully engaged in a kinesthetic way with our entire environment, that we are clearly active and we can begin to tell a story.

We are all just like Alice as we enter the world of the story.
(Illustration by Sir John Tenniel.)

A relationship between two human beings is experienced in space, in time, and in their bodies, through movement. Relationships depend on the exchange of energy between two people, demanding a give-and-take of ideas, thoughts, and, ultimately, emotions. Intimacy can be reached only through personal connection.

The chemical synergy between two human beings is what thrills and engages us as an audience because this is what fuels our own lives. We need each other to successfully exist in our world.

EXPLORATION: WASHING THE FEET

In her book *The Body Speaks*, Lorna Marshall writes, "I always use the idea of a 'task' as a focusing device for emotions. It forces your body to engage with the physical world. Once you have a task, the emotion moves from the abstract realm of thought and memory and enters the concrete territory of the body, which then interacts with tangible reality."

The following exploration involves performing just such a task: washing someone else's feet. The goal of this exercise is to connect to the body during a simple task and to learn that any activity, if done with ease and care, can stimulate a profound level of emotional connection and psychological synergy, joining people in an authentic way.

This process is remarkably simple, yet extremely profound. It helps you experience all the necessary elements for acting truthfully and actively, including connection, awareness, moment-to-moment specificity, presence, and breath. In our "real" world, we rarely experience this. We are all so busy, moving on to the next thing that we have to do and dealing with the distractions that are all around us. We rarely have the time or the solitude to connect to each other in this way.

In the process of this exploration, unfamiliar feelings and emotions may come up. Allow yourself to notice them as they happen. Regardless of what you are feeling, breathe, maintain eye contact with your partner, and continue the task through its conclusion.

NOTE: This exercise should be performed in complete silence.

SETUP

You can do this exploration with two people or with partners within a larger group. The space in which this exploration takes place should not be too brightly lit. The following materials are needed for this exploration:

- A chair

- A bar of soap

- Two bath towels

- A plastic or metal bowl or bucket filled with warm water, large enough to put one of your feet in (we'll refer to this as the *bucket* in the steps that follow)

A simple task like washing the feet, executed with intention and care, becomes a powerful ritual. (Photo: Todd Domenic Cribari.)

EXPLORATION

NOTE: This exploration assumes you are washing your partner's feet.

1. Spread one of the towels on the floor and put the bucket of warm water on the towel. Place the other towel next to the bucket.

2. Have your partner sit on the chair with the towel and bucket of warm water in front of them. Then kneel in front of the bucket, facing your partner.

3. Take one of your partner's feet and carefully place it in the bucket of warm water.

4. Lift your partner's foot out of the water. Then, as you hold it, gently and deliberately wash your partner's foot with the soap.

   Be aware of the contact of your hands with your partner's foot. Take your time. Be thorough. Don't skip any areas of the foot. Sustain a level of alertness and awareness of your body and your breathing.

   TIP: This ritual works best if you maintain eye contact with your partner. And remember: Remain silent.

5. After you have soaped and washed the entire foot, rinse it thoroughly in the bucket. Then, carefully and ceremoniously, remove it from the bucket, place it on one of the towels, and gently dry it completely. Breathe.

6. Place your partner's other foot in the water and repeat the entire process. Don't rush any steps of your careful cleansing. The whole ritual of washing both feet should take about 15 minutes.

7. Empty, rinse, and refill the bucket with warm water.

8. Switch roles in silence and proceed through the ritual again, taking care with every detail.

9. After the exploration is finished, silently and physically give thanks to each other for allowing this experience to take place.

10. Verbally share with each other what you felt and experienced during the process. Be honest about your feelings and observations. If there is a group, gather in a circle, and allow those who would like to share what happened, what they felt, and what they noticed to do so.

REFLECTION

- What was your initial feeling when you first started this exploration?

- How did you feel when you were washing your partner's feet in silence?

- How did you feel when your partner was washing your feet?

- As you were looking at one another, did you sense a different level of communication?

- Did this evoke any feelings or awaken any memories in you?

WATCH THIS MOVIE: *DEPARTURES* (2008)

The Japanese film *Departures* (2008), directed by Yōjirō Takita, provides a perfect example of how a specific task can bring you into the world of the story. *Departures* won the Oscar for best foreign film in 2009.

EXPLORATION: TOP DOG/UNDERDOG

Some people are confident, determined, and clear about the direction of their lives. Some people lack confidence and direction, and move placidly or arbitrarily through their lives.

We call the confident, determined people *top dogs* because they tend to dominate and control their world and the other people in it. They're leaders. In contrast, those lacking confidence and direction—the so-called *underdogs*—tend to follow. Underdogs are ultimately subservient to the top dogs, perhaps lacking the means or the ability to take charge of their destiny.

This hierarchal reality is expressed mentally, emotionally, and physically in the body and in how we move in space. In this exercise, you'll explore how this occurs.

SETUP

This exploration should be done with a large group in a big empty space. The large group should be separated evenly into two smaller groups: Group A (top dogs) and Group B (underdogs).

EXPLORATION

1. Begin the exploration with Group A standing in a line facing one wall and Group B standing in a line facing the opposite wall.

2. Operating in silence, both groups should physically express their emotional and psychological state (Group A, their dominance and superiority, and Group B, their subservience and inferiority). No matter which group you're in, try to identify different ways of standing and moving that will express your status and repeat them so they feel familiar to you.

3. After five minutes of expressing in place, have both groups turn and face each other and move around the room—relating to each other, interacting, and responding to the other "dogs" in the room. Although there should be no talking at this point, participants may express themselves vocally.

> **TIP:** If you are one of the top dogs, it might help you to use the techniques you explored earlier, in the "Dilation of the Body in Space (Kinesphere)" exercise, in which you manifested power and strength through physical elevation and expansion.

4. After 5 or 10 minutes, separate the groups and have them return to their starting point, facing the wall.

5. Have the groups reverse roles, so the top dogs become the underdogs and vice versa. Then repeat the exercise in every detail. Do not skip any steps. Notice how you respond to each other and what new feelings this experience brings about.

6. Have everyone in both groups come together and share how they responded to those who had the power in the room, how this power (or the lack of it) was manifested, and how the differences in the physical and emotional connection were expressed when playing a top dog versus an underdog. This experience should enable every actor to easily switch from a powerful inner and physical state to a weaker and subservient condition.

Expressing the power hierarchy through movement.
(Photo: Todd Domenic Cribari.)

REFLECTION

- How did you feel when you were a top dog?

- How did being a top dog affect the quality, power, and posture of your movement?

- How did you feel when you were an underdog?

- How did being an underdog affect the quality, power, and posture of your movement?

- Were your interactions different when you related to the *top dogs* than when you related to the *underdogs*?

- What was your emotional state? Were you frightened? Exhilarated? Drunk with power?

- Did you find yourself more uncomfortable being the top dog or the underdog? How did this discomfort manifest itself?

- Reflecting on a character you have recently played or worked, would you perceive that character as a top dog or an underdog?

- Which are you in your everyday life—a top dog or an underdog? (Be aware that sometimes we are one in the workplace and the other at home!)

WATCH THESE MOVIES:
ELIZABETH (1998) AND *ANIMAL KINGDOM* (2010)

History has shown that the demeanor of a monarch is essential to successfully (or not) reigning over the political and social functions of a country. In the 1998 film *Elizabeth*, Cate Blanchett's performance is a perfect example of this. Blanchett uses her uncanny skills and talent to embody Elizabeth and to express her development through her physical life. Quite literally, she builds her character's arc with the transformation of the connection between her head and spine, and by emphasizing the dominance of her head over her body. By the end of the film, Elizabeth owns her place on the throne through self-sacrifice and her physical metamorphosis from a young girl into the Virgin Queen—the image of total perfection and absolute power.

Animal Kingdom, which won the World Cinema Jury Prize at the 2010 Sundance Film Festival, stars Jacki Weaver, Ben Mendelsohn, Guy Pierce, Sullivan Stapleton, and James Frecheville, who offer a remarkable example of how the hierarchy of power dominates a crime family in Melbourne. Their family dynamic reminds us of a pack of hyenas led by the matriarch, with a constant struggle for power by the others to become the alpha male. Manipulated by the mother, the ruthless and deadly fight continues to the end.

As Elizabeth I in Elizabeth, *Cate Blanchett conveys her dominance through her poise and regal gait.* (Gramercy Pictures.)

James Frecheville, Jacki Weaver, and Luke Ford in Animal Kingdom. *As the matriarch, Weaver clearly positions herself as the top dog of this family.* (Sony Pictures.)

REVIEW: PART II

After reading Parts I and II and attempting the explorations we have guided you through, you should now be comfortable, and capable of, doing the following:

- Identifying your everyday habits, as well as your habits in performance

- Understanding the principles of the Alexander Technique: awareness, primary control, inhibition, and direction

- Creating and entering a specific space with an awareness of the horizon

- Moving and expanding in the space with an awareness of the specific conditions of your environment

- Making specific choices through memory, history, and all your senses about the objects and furniture in the space

- Relating and responding to the energy and emotions of your scene partners with empathy and physical connectivity

Upon reading this list, if there are any concepts you are not clear about, we recommend you go back and refresh your cognitive and emotional memory before you move on. The information and experiences you have gained throughout this book so far will be most helpful to you if you work at retaining them and bringing each experience you've had with the material to every step of your living process as an actor.

PART III

APPROACHING THE SCRIPT THROUGH CHARACTER

The script is the skeleton of the story. It is the job of the actors, the director, and the artistic team to flesh out this skeleton and give it life; otherwise, every production of a play or version of a movie would be the same.

When you receive a new script, whether it's for a play or a film, you should read it at least three times. The first time you read it, try to forget everything you might know or have heard about the story and characters. Read it without preconceived notions to objectively discover the story, theme, and the writer's intentions. Do not make judgments or endgain results for your character. Your goal should be to understand the story from a neutral point of view so you can see the whole picture.

Reading the script for the first time!

QUESTIONS TO ANSWER AFTER THE FIRST READ

- What is the story about?

- How does the title inform the play or the film?

- What is the theme of the story?

- What is the genre of the story?

- What is the writer's intention in telling this story?

- What is the geographical location and setting?

- What is the historical period in which the story takes place?

- What are the social, political, and cultural characteristics of this period? (You will need to do research to answer this question.)

The second read should be from your character's point of view. Noticing what your character says or does enables you to understand how his or her words and actions affect the events in the story as well as how the events in the story affect him or her. During this second read, pay attention to details so you can answer specific questions about your character's actions, environment, intent, conditions, and so on.

As you learn about your character, consider where and when the story is taking place and question how that might affect the choices you make. To illustrate, let's consider two powerful plays about life and death: Larry Kramer's *The Normal Heart* (2013) and Thornton Wilder's *Our Town* (1940). In both of these plays, people get sick and die, leaving their friends and family to try to cope with and understand the loss—two seemingly timeless themes. The fact that *The Normal Heart* takes place in New York in the early 1980s during the initial outbreak of AIDS in the gay community, whereas *Our Town* is set in a small town in New Hampshire at the turn of the 20th century, drives the characters in these stories to speak, behave, and react to each other very differently. If you placed the action of *The Normal Heart* at the turn of the century in Grover's Corners, New Hampshire, or the action of *Our Town* in New York in the 1980s, neither story would make sense, and the playwright's original intention would be lost.

Matt Bomer and Mark Ruffalo in The Normal Heart. (HBO.)

Martha Scott and William Holden in Our Town.
(United Artists.)

QUESTIONS TO ANSWER AFTER THE SECOND READ

NOTE: You might not find the answers to all these questions in the actual text. Nevertheless, after reading the text, you, as the actor, should be able to infer or create the specific details.

- How does the location of the story affect your character?

- How does the historical period during which the story takes place influence the choices your character makes?

- What did your character's parents do for a living?

- How was your character raised (religion, education, social class, family dynamics, and so on)?

- What is your character's physical appearance and condition (current and past health problems, fitness level, special skills, physical strengths and weaknesses, and so on)?

- What are the most exciting and most traumatic things that have happened to your character—either written in the play or written by you to feed the character's backstory?

- What are the five main qualities of your character?

- How would you describe your character's sex life?

Your third read should focus on character development and on your character's relationship to the other characters in the story. At this point, you, as the character, want to learn what you say about yourself as well as what all the other characters say about you. The first and best tool for understanding your character is the source: the author's words. As you read them, think of yourself as an archaeologist, trying to unearth the evidence and artifacts that clarify and inform who your character is.

Some writers provide a great deal of information about the physicality and emotional background of the characters. In *Death of a Salesman*, Arthur Miller describes Willy Loman like this:

> "From the right, WILLY LOMAN, the Salesman, enters, carrying two large sample cases. The flute plays on. He hears but is not aware of it. He is past sixty years of age, dressed quietly. Even as he crosses the stage to the doorway of the house, his exhaustion is apparent. He unlocks the door, comes into the kitchen, and thankfully lets his burden down, feeling the soreness of his palms. A word-sigh escapes his lips—it might be "Oh, boy, oh, boy." He closes the door, then carries his cases out into the living room, through the draped kitchen doorway."

Other writers furnish little more than the character's name and occupation. For example, in *Marat/Sade* (1967) by Peter Weiss, the description of Rossignol is merely, "a woman of the street."

QUESTIONS TO ANSWER AFTER THE THIRD READ

- What is your character's objective throughout the story, scene by scene, and in relation to the other characters in the story?

- Does your character have a secret? If so, what is it?

- What obstacles must your character overcome to reach his/her objectives, and how does your character do this?

- How does your character change throughout the story?

- What is at stake for your character? How and when does the level of urgency with which they try to reach their objective change throughout the story?

TIP: Time permitting, the most effective way to understand both the role and the script is to read other works by the writer of the script. This will illuminate the writer's style and themes of interest. You might also gain insight from reading literary criticism of the writer's work.

THE CHARACTER BIOGRAPHY AND THE CHARACTER MAP

Using the information you glean from reading the script as a foundation, along with your personal discoveries and feelings about your character as they are informed by events in the story, you will create two critical tools:

- **CHARACTER BIOGRAPHY:** A document about your character

- **CHARACTER MAP:** A visual and sensory construction of the character

Both these tools will help you research, explore, illustrate, and guide a character's psychological and physical makeup, journey, and experience through the story, and to embody the character physically, vocally, emotionally, and spiritually.

> **NOTE:** Researching a character is one of the joys of being an actor. The discoveries you will make about the time and place your character lives in will give you powerful and specific information that will enhance the realism of your performance. In addition, you will develop a life skill and work ethic that will enhance your power as a creative artist.

WRITING A CHARACTER BIOGRAPHY

There are many ways to approach writing your character biography, and the form and style you choose are entirely up to you. For example, you might decide to write it as a journal, a memoir, or random paragraphs, in no particular order, that illustrate key moments in your character's life.

> **NOTE:** Some actors prefer to write biographies of their characters' lives; others prefer to home in on smaller vignettes or snapshots of memories.

Although you can use whatever form and style you choose, we do advise you to write your character biography in the first person and to include specific facts and events that relate to the character's personal history, from childhood to the present. This should include events not mentioned in the actual play. For example, maybe your character has recently seen a great film, eaten a memorable meal, or visited an interesting place. Or maybe they have addictions or health problems. If so, you should tell a story about them. You should also include shared experiences with other characters with which your character has a relationship.

These are just a few suggestions of memories and details you might include. Regardless, having a written document of things your character has experienced to reference during rehearsal will help you to flesh out your character. You'll do more than just act like a certain type of character; you'll embody a living, multidimensional human being with a real history.

> **TIP:** The more specific your character biography is, the better.

CREATING A CHARACTER MAP

The character map is a drawing, collage, or other visual construction that you create that is a visual representation of your character within the story. Your map should contain everything that might influence or be important to your character as well as aspects of your character's emotional composition. Creating a character map will help you bring all the elements and qualities of the character related to rhythm, relationships, physical characteristics, and dreams, to create a fully realized interpretation of the character.

We suggest starting with a large blank poster board or paper. You can then fill this blank surface using, for example:

- Swatches of fabric the character might wear
- Drawings or illustrations of things the character likes to look at
- References to music the character might listen to (which could affect the rhythm and quality of their movement)
- Words or phrases that have special resonance to the character
- Pictures of people the character cares about
- Images of animals that inform the character's physical and spiritual nature

Be sure to include negative qualities in your character map, such as representations of your character's fears, nightmares, addictions, secrets, or failings.

As you create the map, be aware of any turning points in the story that influence or change your character. As you go through the rehearsal process, your character map will help you track your character's evolution.

Don't worry about making a beautiful, perfectly drawn and composed character map. You do not need to be an artist to create an effective character map. Your character map is not something you are creating to show to others. It is a physical representation of images that mean something to you and connect you to your character and the story.

> **TIP:** As you read and rehearse the play or film, start collecting objects, pictures, and artifacts that represent or say something about your character. That way, by the time you start to build your character map, you will have accumulated a collection of items you can use.

Character map created by Kristof Konrad for his character
Dr. Filip Kardel in the short film Breathe *(2015).*

Character map created by Jules Wilcox for her character
Dr. Martha Livingston in the play Agnes of God.

Character map created by Dave Quicksall for his character
of Mercutio in Romeo and Juliet.

Over the years we have seen a wide array of character maps created by actors to reflect who their characters are. Although the character map typically takes the form of drawings or collages, some actors make more elaborate constructions. Here are just a few examples:

- Juliette Binoche, who played the kleptomaniac mother in the film *Bee Season*, created a character map in the form of a shrine made from stolen objects she had taken from the other characters in the story. Throughout the shoot, Binoche frequently referred to this map to find and create Miriam's energy and inner life. It reminded her, in a very visceral way, how each object she stole gave her a sense of life and purpose.

- One actress we know, who played the doctor in Tony Kushner's *Angels in America*, created a character map on a doctor's lab coat, which had a stethoscope, identification tag, blood, pictures of her patients, and a drawing of the virus that causes AIDS.

- Another actress we know, who played amateur sleuth Miss Marple in Agatha Christie's *A Murder Is Announced*, created her character map as a journal/sketchbook, drawing sketches of objects and events that both she, the actress, and she, as Miss Marple, had seen and was struck by. During rehearsal and before performances, in looking at the sketch book, she was able to blend her persona and her character's.

EXPLORATION: USING THE CHARACTER MAP

Making your character map is just the beginning of the process. You should continue to add to and refer to it as you make new discoveries about your character during rehearsals and performances. As you are getting into costume and makeup or warming up, looking at your map will have a powerful and profound effect on your performance because it contains so many keys and prompts about who your character is. It will also help you maintain a level of consistency in your performance. When you are both specific and free in your choices in building your character map, you will find there is a certain alchemy in the relationship between you and the map. This exploration will help you connect with your character map in this way.

SETUP

Find an empty, uncluttered space where you can be alone with your character map—ideally an unoccupied studio, where there are no distractions.

EXPLORATION

1. Place your character map on the floor.

2. Imagine your character in their home or a place where they are comfortable.

3. Choose a simple, mundane task in your character's daily life—preparing to go to bed, getting ready for work, getting ready to meet someone, cleaning up your room, and so on.

4. Study your character map. Observe it in its entirety. Allow each element of the map to inspire and inform how your character accomplishes this very simple task.

5. Begin performing the task as your character. As you do, feel free to make sounds and say a few words or even a line of text. Notice how, due to the influence of the images and feelings conveyed on your character map, the quality of your voice and even your simplest movements differ from how you, as yourself, would usually perform them. (You do not need to make sounds or speak, but if you want to, you can.)

> **TIP:** If your chosen task involves going somewhere, consider what your character takes with them and how they confirm that they have everything they need.

6. When you notice a different quality of a specific movement, repeat it several times so you become aware of how your character performs it. For example, the character might open a door differently

from the way you do—perhaps gripping the knob more tightly and opening the door more carefully. Or maybe the character sits down more slowly and ceremoniously than you would.

> **NOTE:** Even if you integrate only one or two elements from your character map into your task, you will discover that it influences your behavior and physical life, allowing you to experience the task through your character.

REFLECTION

- Did you notice that you found yourself moving in a different way than usual?

- As you referred to your character map, how was the quality of your movement altered? Were your movements faster or slower, bigger or smaller, and so on, than you normally move? Were they more deliberate?

- Were there specific elements from your character map that influenced the quality of your sound and movement? A color? A shape, texture, or text? Was it an animal? Based on this exploration, is there anything you feel compelled to add to your character map?

WORKING WITH CHARACTER ARCHETYPES

Human archetypes are iconic, universally recognized characters that have been used throughout time and across societies. These archetypes appear in mythology, religions, and literature, and throughout the history of theatre. For example, the *commedia dell'arte* included many stock characters, like Arlecchino (the trickster servant), Pantalone (the merchant), Il Dottore (the know-it-all doctor), and various lovers, but there are many other archetypes that we easily recognize and understand.

NOTE: Archetypes should be perceived not as stereotypes, but as complex, multi-layered characters who appear and reappear in the contemporary narratives we continue to create.

EXPLORATION: WORKING WITH ARCHETYPES

There are many archetypes, and we've listed some of them in the following table. (Note: This table was originally conceived by Nigel Jamieson and Frankie Armstrong.) The table also includes the physical center from which each archetype leads and the overall objective that drives them (what they say). The idea is to encourage performers to feel the way in which these physical and emotional centers affect the posture, stance, rhythm, and musicality of the body.

LIST OF ARCHETYPES

ARCHETYPE	WHAT THEY LEAD WITH	WHAT THEY SAY
Child	Forehead	OK (yes to everything)
Virgin	Cheeks	I'm free
Hunter/huntress	Feet	I survive
Warrior	Chest	I conquer
Mother	Hands	I understand
Trickster	Hips	I fool you
Fat man/lady	Tummy	I want more
Crone	Elbows	Is that mine?
Angel/sprite	Shoulder blades	Greeting
Devil	Eyes	I do what I want

> **NOTE:** In our experience, the archetypes listed here work well in virtual environments because they easily evoke a specific physical and vocal expression. For more on virtual environments, see Appendix A, "The Future Is Here: New Technologies."

Encouraging performers to get inside the bodies of these archetypes in space is both challenging and liberating because they experience a kinesthetic response to character development.

SETUP

This exploration can be done in a group or alone. If done in a group, you should position yourselves in a circle so everyone can see each other.

From the chart, choose the archetype you want to explore. Note its name, the body center from which it leads, and its overall objective. (For the purposes of this exploration, we are all going to start with the warrior).

EXPLORATION

1. Stand on your feet, hip-width apart, with your weight evenly distributed on your heels and the balls of your feet. Make sure your feet are parallel to each other, with your big toe and first and second toes facing forward.

2. Remind yourself that you have time.

3. Free your neck to allow your head to go forward and up. Allow your whole body to lengthen and widen and your knees to go forward. Continue this process of directing your body as you perform this exploration.

4. Your center is where the energy that moves or mobilizes your character comes from. It is the source of energy, light, and heat. Because you have chosen the warrior, your main center is in the chest area. You will generate energy, light, and heat from inside your chest.

5. Choose a spot in the room and walk to it, leading with your arche-type's center. (Refer to the preceding table.) Notice how this affects your physicality—your gait, the distribution of weight, and the qual-ity of the movement. Repeat this step and move about the room.

6. As you continue walking about the room, say your objective ("I conquer") out loud. If you are in a group, actually say it to the other people in the room. Do not be surprised if you experience a sense of conflict, since everyone wants to conquer.

7. After a few minutes of exploration, come back to where you started and return to neutral.

8. Let go of the archetype. Release it by becoming a human fountain —using your hands to direct the energy like water up your spine, through the top of your head, and into the atmosphere as the arms come down to the side.

9. Choose a contrasting archetype, such as the mother, and follow the same procedure as before. Feel the energy build and glow from your center as you begin to move and speak your archetype's objec-tive. Continue for no more than two minutes before returning to neutral and repeating the human fountain.

Repeat the entire process with two more archetypes, for a total of four.

REFLECTION

- How do you feel at the end of this process?

- Did you feel the difference between the warrior and the mother? Where did you feel the difference?

- How did being led by different energy centers in your body affect how you moved and spoke?

- After having experienced four different archetypes, are you more aware of your whole body?

> **TIP:** You can use this exploration as you build your character map. It can help you figure out who your character is. Sometimes, you can choose more than one archetype.

RHYTHM AND MUSIC

"Music can lift us out of depression or move us to tears—
it is a remedy, a tonic, orange juice for the ear. But for many of
my neurological patients, music is even more—it can provide access,
even when no medication can, to movement, to speech, to life.
For them, music is not a luxury, but a necessity."

–Oliver Sacks, neurologist

After you have read the play several times, reflected on it, and answered the questions about your character, and created both your character biography and map, you should have a clear idea of who your character is. Now comes the most challenging and crucial step in character development: animating the character and using rhythm to physically bring the character to life.

The nervous system is highly stimulated by our senses of sight and hearing. Our eyes and ears receive fundamental information about the environment that we process to identify our needs and wants. Both the visual and the auditory cortex stir an immeasurable amount of energy in our bodies, and the applications for this energy are infinite.

Much of the information and instructions we are given in our lives is so clear and literal that it limits our choices. But as actors, rather than limit our choices, our *possibilities*, we should expand them. In building a character, the visceral influence of sound and imagery can be a rich source of inspiration and exploration, enabling us to transform ourselves. Actors must thoroughly explore the importance of sound and imagery and how they affect our energy and behavior.

> **NOTE:** This section focuses on using sound—specifically rhythm and music—in constructing our characters; the next one focuses on using imagery.

As humans, rhythm is part of our physiological makeup. Rhythm controls and drives our cardiovascular, respiratory, and digestive systems. There is rhythm in when and how we eat and sleep. When we talk about rhythm, we mean both our own internal rhythm and the rhythms around us. Rhythm colors and informs our movement, behavior, and thought processes.

According to neuroscientist R. Douglas Fields, "Rhythm facilitates people interacting by synchronizing brain waves and boosting performance of perception of what the other person is saying and doing at a particular point in time." Similarly, psychologist Annett Schirmer observes that when we see an image, it creates a brain wave that excites the whole neuromuscular system, but when the image is presented simultaneously with a rhythm, the electrical response evoked by the image is bigger.

The power of music and rhythm to tap into our brain circuits and control emotion and movement also controls the brain circuitry of sensory perception. According to Fields, "This discovery helps explain how drums unite tribes in ceremony, why armies march to drum and bugle into battle, why worship and ceremonies are infused by song, why speech is rhythmic, punctuated by rhythms of emphasis on particular syllables and words, and perhaps why we dance."

This section explores rhythms that affect our whole mind, body, and spirit, enabling actors to create fully delineated, living, breathing human beings. Inspired by rhythms, we describe the fundamental rhythms that are always present in our lives and that inform all our actions:

- **QUIET:** This describes an experience of ease, quietness, and calm. It is the pause before action—but also the movement underneath. Think about looking at still water from a distance. It might appear to be calm on the surface, but underneath, there are currents, turbulence, and life—always moving and active.

Musically, "quiet" could be conveyed through meditative music, chanting, or long and sustained chords.

- **UNDULATE:** This is an effortless, gentle movement that awakens the body into activity. It is the gentle breeze that blows a fallen leaf, the swell of an ocean before a wave breaks, the force that builds toward excitement. Musically, "undulate" is exemplified by genres such as samba, bossa nova, or hula.

- **ABRUPT:** This refers to an energetic, percussive rhythm that stimulates the whole system. Imagine the sights and sounds that precede the Roman army marching—an orchestra of drums and trumpets heralding the arrival of the most powerful army in the world. Musically, "abrupt" can be found in rock and roll, a drum line, the music played at a gym, or anything that speeds the heart.

- **HAVOC:** This is an incessant, out-of-control beat that eventually explodes. Imagine Times Square at rush hour or an anarchic battlefield. Musically, it is a compilation of dissonant and disparate sounds—heavy metal, Stravinsky, and dubstep.

- **PEACE:** After the climax of havoc inevitably comes peace—the calm after the storm. It is the moment of forgiveness and coming together after conflict when resolution is achieved. Musically, it might be expressed by a legato symphony with violins playing long phrases, as in a Bach adagio.

These universal rhythms can be found in many aspects of our lives—the chronological stages of our lives, our romantic and sexual relationships, the progression of a story, and so on. Think about the stages of a courtship: quiet is the first attraction, undulate is escalating flirtation, abrupt is the act of sex, havoc is achieving and reaching climax, and peace is the afterglow.

The exercises and explorations in this section will tap into these five rhythms and connect you to your nervous system and to the main thing that drives all your actions: your primitive gut response. *Gut response* is not just an expression. There is an actual nerve, the vagus nerve, that connects from the brain all the way down to the visceral area and controls ingestion, digestion, assimilation, and elimination, as well as the heart and lungs. The communication between the brain to the vagus nerve is constant—so much so that this nerve acts like a primitive, second brain that responds to sudden danger, fear, and emotions. So, when you say, "I have a gut feeling about this," you literally do.

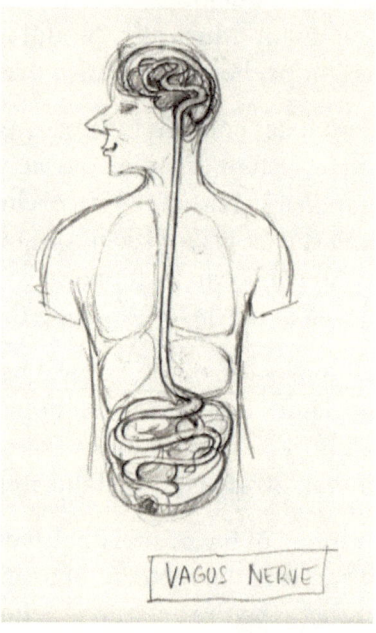

"I have a gut feeling about this...."
The vagus nerve connects your brain to your stomach.

NOTE: For an actor, understanding the connection between your two brains and the balanced use of the self is invaluable. Without it, there will always be a sense of incompleteness and a lack of confidence in exploring the unknown.

EXPLORATION: THE FUNDAMENTAL RHYTHMS

Now that you are aware of these rhythms, the following explorations will enable you to integrate them into your body and your nervous system as you move through space.

SETUP

Create a playlist for this exploration. This playlist should include one song or musical piece for each of the rhythms. Here is a sample playlist that we have used in the past:

- **QUIET:** "No Place Nowhere" by David Darling
- **UNDULATE:** "Lola's Lullaby" by Anoushka Shankar
- **ABRUPT:** "Saltarello" by Dead Can Dance
- **HAVOC:** Gorecki's "Kleines Requiem" by Reinbert De Leeuw
- **PEACE:** Mahler's "Symphony No. 5 in C Sharp Minor" by Daniel Barenboim

After you create your playlist, find a large, empty space that is big enough for people to move in freely, preferably with a hardwood floor. You will need an audio player and powerful speakers to play and amplify the playlist. Ideally, you should perform this exercise in a group or at least with a partner. If you are doing this in a group, have someone act as a leader to guide you.

Actors connecting to each other through rhythm. (Photo: Todd Domenic Cribari.)

EXPLORATION

> **NOTE:** This is a silent exploration. There should be no speaking for the duration.

1. Lie on the floor on your back, at rest, with your eyes closed and your arms and legs spread out.

2. Play the music.

3. Slowly get up. For the sake of safety, open your eyes, but do not focus on what others are doing.

4. As the music that represents the first rhythm, quiet, plays, allow your body to move and respond spontaneously to the rhythm and feeling of the music. Do not plan, judge, or choreograph your movement. Your only direction is to move as the music inspires you to.

> **NOTE:** Although others may be moving in a very different way than you are, do not let yourself be influenced by them—only by the music.

5. Between each of the pieces, there will be a brief pause, allowing you to rest and transition to the next rhythm.

6. As the music for the second rhythm, undulate, begins, find a partner. Establish eye contact to connect with them. Remain connected to this partner, your eyes locked, for the remainder of the exploration as you move through each rhythm.

> **NOTE:** This is not a mirror exercise, so when moving in partnership, do not feel you have to move as your partner does. Move only as the music inspires *you* to move—but together.

7. When the music ends, stop moving, and share a moment of acknowl-edgment or gratitude with your partner. Then return to stillness.

8. Take a break, hydrate, and let your heart rate slow back down.

9. Gather with the rest of the group to reflect on what you experienced during the exploration. This is not a conversation; it is a chance for each person to briefly share what they felt.

REFLECTION

- Did each rhythm inspire you to move in a different way? If yes, how?

- Were some rhythms easier to move to than others? Why?

- Did certain rhythms help you use more of your body?

- Did you use more space with some of the rhythms? Which ones?

- As your musical rhythm and the quality of your movement changed, did you feel any different emotions?

- Did this exploration stimulate your imagination? Did you find yourself transforming into a different character or an animal?

- As you were inspired by and moving to these five rhythms, did you feel at any point that you were living in a story? What was the story about?

EXPLORATION: THE SOUNDTRACK OF OUR LIVES

Much of what we do, how we live, and how we move is driven by the fundamental rhythms. But regardless of what the rhythms are, there seems to always be music around us in all aspects of our lives—whether we are driving in a car, walking by a house, shopping in a mall, stand-ing in an elevator, and so on. This exploration explores how different genres and rhythms of music can influence how we feel and move.

SETUP

Create a playlist containing between 10 and 15 excerpts from different songs, both sung and orchestral, blending as many contrasting styles as you can. The playlist should be about 20 minutes long, with many different styles. Here is a sample playlist we have used; you can use this or make your own:

- Prokofiev's "Symphony No. 1 in D major, Op. 25"
- "Comedy Tonight" from *A Funny Thing Happened On the Way to the Forum*
- "Overture" from *Out of Africa*
- "Main Title" from *A Streetcar Named Desire*
- "Little Drummer Boy" by Marlene Dietrich
- "Life Is" from *Zorba*
- Juicing infomercial (you could use any commercial or spoken word piece for this)
- "Timber Trail" by Sons of the San Joaquin
- "James Bond Theme" by John Barry & Orchestra
- "March of the Children" from *The King and I*

You will need an audio player and powerful speakers to play and amplify the playlist you created to accompany this exploration.

You can do this exploration alone or in a group. Either way, choose a simple household task or chore to complete silently during the exploration. The duration of this task should be 10 to 12 minutes, and there should be many components: setting the table and preparing for dinner, cleaning up one's room, washing the car, gardening, and so on. It should not be a single task, such as sweeping or mowing a lawn.

A VARIATION...

During this exploration, often we do a guided narration at certain points, prompting the participants to alter their activity or introducing new information or stimuli to enhance the exploration. For instance, we might throw in a twist like, "It's very hot, and you're very tired; take a break to have a glass of cold lemonade." Then, "Now that you are refreshed, how does this alter your behavior in the performance of your task?"

As the last phase of music begins, we might inform the participants that their task is complete, that they have done a marvelous job, and that the emperor is coming on horseback to honor them for completing their task. The participants continue moving, influenced by the music—only now they are no longer doing their task, but are instead readying themselves for the emperor's visit.

EXPLORATION

1. Perform the task. Many people can do their tasks at the same time. Although they are in the same space, they should not interact with each other.

2. Have the music start about 30 seconds into the task. Let the music guide the quality of your movement. Do what the music moves you to do. At any point, you may stop to take a break, but continue to allow the music to influence how you move and behave.

REFLECTION

- How did you feel throughout this exploration?

- How did the change in tone and spirit of each selection of music alter how you approached your task?

- Did you find yourself moving in different ways, even though you were doing the same task throughout the exploration?

- Reflect on or share with the other participants which part of the music affected you most deeply and how it changed your perspective.

- Were there times when the music compelled you to abandon your task and do something else?

> **TIP:** From now on, in your daily life, try to notice if and how the music you hear influences the quality of your movement and how you feel.

ANIMATING IMAGES

Just as you are influenced and surrounded by different sounds, music, and rhythms, you are also influenced by images in every area of your life. These images shape and affect you, whether consciously or unconsciously.

As the Jungian psychologist Marion Woodman remarked in her 2016 book *Conscious Femininity*:

> "Images are pictures of the soul and we use those as the bridge between psyche and the body...The point is we are flesh and blood and often we don't experience the reality of psychic image until we feel it in our body."

Nebuchadnezzar by William Blake.
Images are an effective tool in creating a character.

Similarly, Konstantin Stanislavski's practice of responsive interaction is based on the connection between the mind and the body—that is, the mind seeing an image causes an effect in your body and evokes a physical response.

Imagery is a powerful way of bridging the imagination and the body. Without imagery, actors' choices tend to be dry and stereotypical. Harnessing the power of imagery will help you to find different tones, colors, and complexities in your work that, otherwise, would be lacking.

EXPLORATION: ANIMATING AN IMAGE

For this exploration, you will use images and music to reflect on a scene in a play you have read several times. Be sure you understand the whole play, have a sense of the story arc, and connect all the relationships of the characters.

We have found this exercise to be enormously freeing and creative for most actors. It allows you to distance yourself from the habitual and literal and to enter into the world of the unexpected and the fantastic, where anything is possible.

Free yourself from the habitual and literal. (Shane Rounce.)

SETUP

Find several images that represent or reflect the scene you have chosen. These images should be inspirational rather than literal. They could be a metaphor for the play, event, or character. It is crucial that you see some aspect of the main character within at least some of the images you have chosen—even if it is only a color, a face, or a landscape that represents the character.

> **TIP:** If you cannot find any images that fully satisfy you, create some. If you like, draw or paint your ideal image or make a collage of images from magazines or the internet.

Then, you need to choose a piece of music to animate your image. Rhythm is essential in giving the scene and the character action and purpose. The genre can be anything (jazz, classical, hip-hop, world music, and so on) as long as it serves the storytelling, the world of the play, and the specific quality of the character. Try to use instrumental music rather than music that contains vocals, so it doesn't distract you.

This exercise is best done in an empty studio, preferably with a hardwood floor. You can do it alone or in a small group. (If your image contains more than one person, invite other participants to join in.) You will need an audio player and powerful speakers to play and amplify the music that accompanies this exploration, and a pen and paper to write down your thoughts afterward.

EXPLORATION

1. Study your image in great detail. Allow every cell of your body to respond to what you see. Keep the image on the floor or on a chair, where you can see it.

2. Play your piece of music and allow yourself to move to it for the first time. Make no effort to maintain the image in your conscious mind. Instead, allow the music and the image to meld together. Let them

integrate into action within the space in a spontaneous way. Do not rehearse or repeat this process; you will lose the spontaneity and sense of discovery of the experience.

> **NOTE:** Be aware this is not dancing as we understand it, but rather a raw form of expression that is much more connected to the subconscious, or the "gut-brain" mentioned earlier.

When you have finished moving, pause and say to yourself, "I have time." Feel all the sensations in your body. Take note of the dominant emotion you are experiencing. As you reflect, write about what you have discovered.

REFLECTION

- How did the music help you to bring your image to life?

- Did a story emerge from the integration of the image and the music? If so, what kind of story was it?

- How did the integration of the image and the music help free you from overthinking?

- Did the rhythm of the music provide energy and a forward-moving impulse to tell your story?

- Did you feel freer in space and in your body?

- Did the integration of the music and the image work together to integrate your body and your spirit in your response?

KEEP ME WILD: THE ANIMAL WITHIN

The presence and power of animals in human civilizations have existed since the dawn of time. Even now there exists in us an ever-present hunger to connect with nature and animals. Throughout history, societies have chosen particular animals as symbols to represent their strengths, positions, or beliefs. For example, the United States has an eagle, Russia a bear, and Venice a lion with wings. It's no surprise, then, that experiencing the world through the eyes, perspective, and body of an animal will help you find your character's reality, shape, and power. Indeed, when we work with actors, we *always* rely on animal movement studies to help them discover and animate their character.

The Lion of St. Mark is an excellent example of the winged lion, symbolically representing the power of Venice as an economic center of Europe between 1500 and 1800.

(Image: "The Lion of St. Mark" [detail] by Vittore Carpacci. Tempera on canvas. Palazzo Ducale, Venice.)

Animal comes from the root word *animalis,* which means having breath or soul. As civilized as we think we are, we still have the same basic physiological and neurological responses as animals when we are confronted with various stimuli: hunger, fear, and threats to our survival. We also share the need for family bonding, play, and procreation.

In his 1997 book *Waking the Tiger,* Peter A. Levine expresses our animal essence and connection in the following way:

> "The foundation for human physiology evolved with the earliest creatures that crawled out of the primordial ooze. As much as we would like to think otherwise, our connection to that beginning has remained fundamentally the same."

Another reason we study animals as a fundamental step when building a character is that all animals are at one with their environment. They are constantly receiving and sending messages, and they are always attuned to their world—fighting for their territory and risking their lives to survive.

In The Berliner Ensemble's production of Bertolt Brecht's The Resistible Rise of Arturo Ui, *the actor playing Arturo Ui, Martin Wuttke, embodies a dog, panting and drooling in hunger with his bright red tongue hanging out— a textbook example of using animal work to express a character.*
(Courtesy of Jerry Telfer, San Francisco Chronicle/Polaris.)

Animals give us a direct link to truth and help us complete our transformation into a character. They are natural guides to accessing our own innate energies to create a full and active human being. Studying animals has helped many actors discover new ways of approaching and building a character—for example, Brando using the qualities of a gorilla in his portrayal of Don Corleone in *The Godfather*, Juliette Binoche, those of a hummingbird in *Bee Season*, and Leonardo DiCaprio, a hawk in *J. Edgar*.

CHARLES LE BRUN

Charles Le Brun (1619–1690) was a prominent painter and artist who drew curious physiognomy studies between humans and animals. Viewing these can help you see how animals can be used to create characters.

Drawings from Resemblances, Amazing Faces *by Charles Le Brun (1619–1690).*

ANIMAL INTELLIGENCE AND INDIGENOUS CULTURES

In American Indian cultures, animals are used to elevate the human spirit, to transcend our daily life into an extraordinary and transformative experience—all we would wish in a theatrical or film performance.

Noted anthropologist, Jeremy Narby, author of the acclaimed books *Intelligence in Nature* and *The Cosmic Serpent*, has studied shamanistic rituals in the Amazon Basin for 25 years, including the use of ayahuasca, a psychedelic brew of plant infusions used by indigenous people for healing and for coping with physical and mental illness. When people ingest *ayahuasca*, they can override their rational brain and experience the world as the animal that they are. So, when the participants in these rituals are under the influence of ayahuasca, their neocortex—the rational thinking brain that filters our judgment and our choices—is bypassed. Of this "animal intelligence," Narby observed in a 2009 interview with Jean-Louis:

> "One of the things that is surprising to the rational mind who is actually sitting there in the back seat, [is that] it's almost scary how intelligent the body is. Most of the time the neocortex is blocking out the intelligence, but the body is an animal. We are animals but our rational mind cuts ourselves off from the animal and in these modified states of consciousness the animal gets back in the driver's seat and hey, he's a pretty good driver, way more attuned to many more fundamental things. If we wanted to figure out the engine of a space rocket we ask the rational mind to do it. But for day-to-day getting along in the world, even if you're only dealing with human beings, other human beings are animals. If you use your animal intelligence to deal with other human animals, you have more tools in your pocket."

Patrick Stewart as Prospero in The Tempest. *In this RSC production, Prospero was a Shaman with animal powers.* (Courtesy of Alastair Muir.)

As actors, our rational human brain does not always serve us well. The following animal explorations will help you to get out of your human head and into your animal body in a visceral and urgent way—and without the use of ayahuasca! These explorations are not merely exercises to use as a jumping-off point to discover and create your character. If you remain acutely aware of the defining characteristics of the animal you associate with your character throughout the rehearsal process and your performance, that animal will become seamlessly integrated into the fabric of your character.

JEAN-LOUIS

In the film *Citizen Gangster* (2012), based on a true story, Scott Speedman portrays Depression-era Canadian bank robber Edwin Boyd. A WWII veteran, Boyd had failed to realize his dream of becoming a Hollywood actor and struggled to find work to provide for his wife and child. Boyd became a bank robber, living a dual life as a loving family man and a flamboyant outlaw.

In preparing for the role, Speedman came to me to help him become freer in his body so he could successfully integrate Boyd's physical, emotional, and psychological complexities. Speedman knew that Boyd had treated his burglaries as performances; before he robbed a bank, Boyd put on makeup as a means of getting into "character." Speedman decided that when Boyd donned the persona of the bank robber, he would become fox-like. He studied the movement and behavior of the fox and channeled its movement, alertness, and playfulness into Boyd.

I worked with Speedman to explore how Boyd would don his bank-robber persona. With his character map laid on the floor, we worked to modulate the balance between fox and human. Speedman started all fox and zero human, then 75 percent fox and 25 percent human, then 50 percent fox and 50 percent human. It was at this point that I asked him to go to the table where the makeup was laid out. To facilitate his exploration of becoming "the robber," I put on music that reflected his sense of the character and what was happening at this moment in the story.

Speedman responded to the music as he carefully applied the makeup. Then I saw him transform before my eyes. He stood up and started moving like a fox around the space. We set up furniture to approximate the counter of a bank teller window and he danced on it before vaulting over it. It was at this moment that he found Edwin Boyd's outlaw persona.

Scott Speedman used a fox as a base to play Canadian bank robber Edwin Boyd in Citizen Gangster. (Entertainment One.)

It was when Scott Speedman applied makeup to create the "mask" of his robber, that he transformed both physically and spiritually into the fox.
(Left Photo: Courtesy of Roeselien Raimond; Right Photo: Entertainment One.)

WATCH THESE MOVIES: *CITIZEN GANGSTER* (2012) AND *A STREETCAR NAMED DESIRE* (1951)

Scott Speedman's performance in *Citizen Gangster* (2012) film is the quintessential example of how, through the integration of all of your understanding of your character's history and circumstances, the character map, animal behavior, rhythm, and physicality, you can create a vivid, multi-layered, and riveting character. Watching the film, you can almost imagine Boyd with the tail of a fox every time he vaults over a bank counter!

In *A Streetcar Named Desire* (1951), Marlon Brando plays Stanley Kowalski, a brutish, blue-collar working man. Brando chose a silver-backed gorilla as his main animal, which worked for most of Stanley's behavior and actions. But just as every person cannot be defined by just one quality, Stanley has many facets, including a sensitive side. Perhaps Brando also chose an eager-to-please and innocent puppy to color how he relates to Stella and his anticipation of his imminent role as a father, as well as to show the pain he feels from the verbal and psychological abuse he receives at Blanche's hands.

Marlon Brando as Stanley Kowalski with Vivien Leigh as Blanche DuBois in A Streetcar Named Desire. *Brando based his character's physicality and aggressive behavior on an ape.*

EXPLORATION: ENTERING THE BODY OF THE ANIMAL

Engaging in animal studies is a fundamental step toward transforming yourself into a character. To feel the animal's inner life, your body must be able to respond physically, like an animal.

For this exploration, you will choose a character. This character could be one you are creating for a specific role or project or one from a classical or contemporary play or film. You will then identify an animal that is like the character you have selected. Perhaps a particular animal will immediately come to mind. If not, consider your character's personality, shape, and physical qualities, and think about what animal—it could be an elephant, a lion, a fish, an insect, a bird, a snake, or something else—also possesses these qualities.

After you choose your animal, observe and study its behavior, movement, and environment. The best way to do this is to observe them in their natural habitat. If this is impossible, try viewing them at a zoo. This will enable you to sense, smell, listen to, and learn about the animal in its environment.

> **TIP:** You can also study your animal by watching videos. Thanks to YouTube, not only can you watch any animal you can imagine, but you can observe them in action, at rest, eating, and so on. However, try not to rely on video. There's no real substitute for observing an animal in person.

As you observe the animal, take photographs, videos, and notes as well as making drawings. Your observation of the animal should be specific and detailed, and include the following elements:

- Rhythm
- Shape/outline
- Weight

- Texture

- Color

- Gaze

- Temperature

- Sounds

- Relationship to the environment (ocean, desert, jungle, and so on)

- Relationship to others

- Behavioral and dietary habits

- Movement qualities (for example, crawling, hopping, or flowing)

> **NOTE:** Observing the animal for only 10 minutes is not going to help you. Careful observation takes time and energy. This is crucial to the effectiveness of this exploration.

When you put in the time and effort to research and observe your animal, and commit to using all of yourself in transforming your body, mind, and spirit into the animal, you will come out of this exploration with specific and practical revelations regarding how to embody your character using the qualities of your animal. This may not be the case for everyone the first time they attempt this exploration, however. If you did not spend enough time observing the animal, or if you did not fully commit to being the animal, you may find yourself end-gaining during the exploration, wondering what you're supposed to do and whether you're doing it right. If so, you probably need to observe and research the animal more deeply and try the exploration again.

> **NOTE:** Only after you truly connect with, and transform yourself, both physically and spiritually into your animal, will you be able to effectively use what you have learned from being the animal in your character work.

In Life of Pi, *Suraj Sharma studied tiger behavior to inhabit the tiger from the inside, merging authentically with the tiger from his head to his spine.*
(20th Century Fox.)

SETUP

Find an empty space that is large enough for people to move in freely, preferably with a hardwood floor. If you are working in a large studio, consider using mats, cubes, or benches to create uneven terrain.

You may do this alone or as a group. If you are doing this as a group, the first time you transform into and experience becoming your animal, we recommend not relating to the other animals around you. There will be time for that later. Once you are more familiar with your animal, your interactions with other animals will be more authentic.

> **TIP:** If becoming your animal involves crawling on the floor, it might be wise to use knee pads or protective padding.

EXPLORATION

1. Stand with your feet hip-width apart. Look down at your feet. If they are turned out, slowly move your heels out until your feet are more parallel and your knees are released over your big toe. Tell yourself, "I have time." Take the time to observe the whole landscape of your body balancing in space and in relationship from your head down to the feet.

2. Applying the Alexander Technique, release your neck. Allow your head to go forward and up, your body to lengthen and widen, and your knees to release forward. Repeat this series of directions a few times, not looking for results or an end product but instead trusting in the process and absorbing your body's directional energy.

3. Notice your breathing. If you are holding your breath, exhale. Just by allowing your breath to come out, the next breath will come in on its own accord.

4. Leading with your head, allow your spine to lengthen as you morph into the body of your animal. Allow this morphing process to take time. Feel the animal's spine, vertebra by vertebra, and slowly take the animal's shape.

   When we speak of "shape," we mean whether the animal is standing on two or four feet, or is a bird perched on a branch or a crocodile floating in the water. Your animal could be a dolphin or a snake. The unusual shapes of these animals will take your nervous system by surprise. You might even discover muscles and feelings you have never experienced before.

5. Consider the specific elements we asked you to notice while you were observing your animal—rhythm, weight, texture, color, gaze, temperature, sounds, and the relationship to your environment.

6. Begin moving in your environment, keeping in mind how your animal moves in its world—crawling, hopping, or flying.

   This process of transforming into the shape and structure of the animal and moving as the animal's body represents an enormous learning for any actor. This process engages and integrates the whole person.

7. Start using your senses as the animal, looking at your world as your animal would. What do you smell? What sounds do you hear in the distance? Take these sensory stimuli in, stretching out your spine and then your limbs and feeling the physical texture of the environment.

8. Sense the taste in your mouth. Move your tongue the way your animal would and make a sound. Repeat the sound several times. Allow it to vibrate through your body. Let it grow in intensity, and then become quiet again.

9. As you move as your animal, explore the space in which you are living. Be very specific in using all your senses. Animals are always attuned to the space they call home. It is their territory, and they must protect it, live in it, and mark it with their scent.

10. Respond as the animal to sounds you are hearing, objects you are encountering, smells you are noticing, and tastes you are experiencing. Animals are always in the moment. They can pay attention to a single sight or sound for lengthy periods of time.

11. Explore moving and experiencing life as your animal for at least 20 minutes. This should include sleeping.

> **TIP:** You might find it rewarding to do it for longer periods as you gain greater flexibility, strength, and familiarity with your animal. It takes time for this process to work its magic!

12. When you are ready to return to human form, slowly and calmly allow your head to lead your spine up until you are standing, continuing to breathe as you do.

> **NOTE:** This exercise opens your entire nervous system, making you much more vulnerable than you are in your everyday life. That is why it is important to enter and exit the body of the animal slowly and gently.

13. To release any tension you may have accumulated during this exercise, lead your arms up by your fingers and breathe out through the top of your head as if water is spouting out of it. Then allow your arms to expand out to the side and come back down. Repeat this several times; finish by shaking out your arms and legs.

Physicality, behavior, and movement: These actors have completely transformed into their chosen animals. (Photo: Todd Domenic Cribari.)

REFLECTION

- How did you feel? Did you find it physically challenging to alter your physical shape and the quality of your movement to that of your animal?

- What, specifically, did you do to change your body into the animal's body?

- Were you able to perceive your environment through the animal's eyes and consciousness?

- Did the animal's consciousness drive and control your behavior —your gaze, your gestures, the power and energy of your gait, and so on?

- What did you identify as the main qualities of your animal that you could incorporate most effectively into the physical and behavioral qualities of your character?

EXPLORATION: ADDING MUSIC AND TEXT

The most beneficial way to bridge the transition between your animal and your character is by adding music and text. This will enable you to maintain the animal qualities you discovered and explored in the previous exercise and facilitate bringing those qualities into your character in the play or scene.

As we explained earlier, rhythm can be helpful in discovering a character's life and overall intention in the play. Everyone has a specific rhythm connected to the drumbeat of their lives; animals also have a very definitive pace and rhythm.

For this exploration, which you should attempt only after you have completed the previous one, you will choose a piece of music you feel expresses the rhythm of your animal and your character. The style of music you select does not matter, as long as it generates an authentic response from you in movement and helps animate the animal and, through it, your character. The music should be instrumental without lyrics.

In addition to choosing a piece of music, memorize one of your character's monologues (a short one) or a few lines that your character says. Be sure to identify keywords or phrases that serve as hooks or anchors for your character. Photocopy the monologue or series of lines onto a single sheet of paper and place it somewhere that you can see it.

Once you are comfortable physically embodying your animal, adding music and text will connect you to your character in the scene. Here, actor Michael N. Kühl becomes a panther. (Photo: Myrna Makaroon.)

SETUP

Find an empty space that is large enough for people to move in freely, preferably with a hardwood floor. If you are working in a large studio, consider using mats, cubes, or benches to create uneven terrain. You will also need someone who can turn on your music for you.

This exploration should be done one person at a time. Each actor will have different music for their animal.

> **TIP:** If becoming your animal involves crawling on the floor, it might be wise to use knee pads or protective padding.

EXPLORATION

1. Stand with your feet hip-width apart. Free your neck so your head perches on the top of your spine. Aim the top of your head to the sky and allow your spine to follow, lengthening and widening your whole torso. Be sure your knees are free and are released forward.

2. Slowly enter the body of your animal by allowing your head to lead your spine into the animal's shape. Be aware of your animal's head-to-tail relationship and notice how the head-to-spine direction gives both form and weight to your animal.

3. Use your senses. See, smell, taste, and touch the world as your animal. Be aware of how you are moving, how you are connected to the ground and the environment, and how you are observing your surroundings from inside your animal mind.

4. Have someone start the music and slowly let it guide your movement in space. React as your animal, without analyzing what you are doing, only responding to the vital rhythm.

5. As you continue moving with the music, make full use of the space, exploring new areas of the room. As you do, consider what heightened senses, strengths, and abilities your animal has, and whether you perceive any threats or find anything attractive. Completely

explore every possible experience of the animal, letting the music influence the pace, rhythm, and quality of the movement.

6. When you feel you have thoroughly inhabited the animal in space, continue moving, and begin making sounds as the animal.

7. Transition into saying several lines of the text as the animal. Repeat a specific sentence or, if you can, recite the entire monologue. Do not concern yourself with the humanity of the character; at this point, you are simply being the animal.

   Connect the tone and energy of your animal sounds to the lines of text. Try sustaining the sounds and vocal qualities of the animal as you recite the lines. Although you are putting energy and focus into channeling the animal vocally, be sure you continue to incorporate the animal's physicality, as well. This should last between 10 and 15 minutes.

8. Once you feel you *are* the animal, continue to say lines from the text, and begin integrating your animal with your human, bipedal self. Slowly bring yourself up onto your feet but continue to breathe, move, and exist as the animal. You are the essence of the animal, breathing in its rhythm, moving with its qualities, but you now have the ability to walk on two feet, pick things up with your hands, and speak. It is as if your animal woke up today in a human body.

9. Continue to speak your lines in this upright position as you move around. See how the lines change as you transform from 100 percent animal to 50 percent animal and 50 percent human. At this point, you are trying to merge the human character with the animal that is driving the character.

10. Continue moving and speaking while blending the animal and human and start playing with the percentages. Try being 50 percent animal and 50 percent human, 30 percent animal and 70 percent human, and 20 percent animal and 80 percent human.

    Through exploration and experimentation, you will discover the most effective ratio of animal-to-human qualities for your role and story. Your objective is to use the animal's qualities to convey the animal essence of your character without being cartoonish or so over the top that you do not seem like a real person.

TIP: It might be beneficial for you to repeat this exploration as an animal you feel is most *unlike* your character. Judiciously adding elements of this contrasting animal will enable you to deliver a fuller, more complex performance as your character.

REFLECTION

- When the music came on, how did that alter your movement pattern, rhythm, tempo, weight, and energy as you were being your animal?

- Were you able to incorporate the quality of the animal sound into the way you spoke the lines while still sustaining the physicality of the animal?

- What did you experience when you were moving as the animal while speaking the text?

- How did the animal's main qualities manifest themselves in the tone of your voice and your speech pattern?

- As you experimented with the ratio of animal-to-human energy, did you find a different buoyancy and flexibility within your body?

- Having done these explorations, did you find the animal you chose served you in developing your character?

TIP: If you feel like your animal moved you in a direction that does not feel appropriate to the character, choose a different animal and repeat the exploration.

PLAYING PHYSICAL AND EMOTIONAL DIFFERENCES

There are many roles that call for having a physical difference, either through disease, trauma or accident, birth defect, addiction, emotional impairment, or just appearance. Playing any of these kinds of characters takes a great deal of skill and self-awareness and presents incredible opportunities and challenges in exploring ways of moving that are foreign to us but, ultimately, are enlightening and powerful.

As we said in Part I, "The Alexander Technique and the Actor," an actor needs to discover, accept, and understand their habitual physical behaviors. You can employ the Alexander Technique to use your body to its maximum efficiency, enabling you to first find your neutral self in order to play someone with extreme physical challenges. The Alexander Technique is equally valuable to actors *with* disabilities.

> **NOTE:** Major institutions such as the National Theatre in London have come out with strong statements regarding authentic casting policies for disabled roles. We hope this trend will continue as more theatres and production companies around the world adopt these policies.

There are many stories, both in film and theatre, where the protagonist is either physically or emotionally impaired. This aspect of these characters calls for specialized preparation—physically, emotionally, and intellectually—to create the realistic illusion of dealing either with physical or emotional constraints.

Eddie Redmayne as Stephen Hawking in *Theory of Everything* (2014), Channing Tatum and Steve Carell in *Foxcatcher* (2014), and Bradley Cooper in a 2014 revival of *The Elephant Man* demonstrated a remarkable ability to transform themselves, with great specificity and authenticity, into different kinds of people. Similarly, the characters in Sting's musical *The Last Ship*—working men who are marginalized and robbed of their livelihoods and identities as their shipyard closes—are damaged, though not as clearly physically or emotionally challenged as those we just mentioned. All these actors found ways to embody these conditions while still showing tremendous depth and humanity.

In the play *The Elephant Man*, the main character, John Merrick, is released from captivity as a freak in a circus sideshow, where he has been terribly mistreated. Despite this, and despite his enormous deformity, he is able to find a positive outlook in his situation. His willingness to open himself and learn gives him the humanity to relate to other characters in the story as a person, not as an outcast.

WATCH THESE MOVIES: *THEORY OF EVERYTHING* (2014) AND *FOXCATCHER* (2014)

To play Stephen Hawking, Eddie Redmayne spent four months researching the life of the famous physicist who suffered from amyotrophic lateral sclerosis (ALS), a progressive and fatal disease that attacks the parts of the brain that control voluntary movement. To map out the physical progression of Hawking's disease, Redmayne watched videos and read books about Hawking, visited a clinic that specialized in caring for ALS patients, and trained with movement director Alex Reynolds. This enabled him to authentically represent Hawking's physical condition throughout the course of his debilitation. To ensure that he expressed every detail in his facial mannerisms and behavior, Redmayne also watched documentary footage of Hawking while sitting in front of a mirror, allowing him to accurately manifest Hawking's physical condition. By the time Redmayne actually met Hawking, it was just five days before he began shooting, so he had already done most of his preparation. The power of Redmayne's performance lies not just in how he embodied Hawking's physical reality, but in how he revealed the man's light, energy, and humor.

Eddie Redmayne won an Oscar for his physical embodiment of Steven Hawking's declining health in The Theory of Everything.
(Focus Features.)

As Steven Hawking, Eddie Redmayne depicts a man who is psychologically healthy but experiencing the effects of advancing ALS. In contrast, as Mark Schultz in *Foxcatcher*, Channing Tatum portrays someone who has a strong, healthy body but is *emotionally* undeveloped—capturing Schultz's innocence and naivete but also the physical reality of a gold medal–winning Olympic wrestler. Ultimately, Tatum uses extreme physicality to mask his vulnerability and lack of confidence.

To achieve this, Tatum and Mark Ruffalo—who portrays Mark Schultz's brother, David—trained at a gym for three months, practicing the moves and skills of freestyle wrestlers. This not only informed their athletic relationship but also their dependent relationship as brothers.

From the very start of the film, Tatum conveys that he is an Olympic wrestler. He uses everyday physical activities (walking, eating, handling objects, gathering his bag, setting up his toaster, and so on) to inform his character. He does not play dumb, but the way he speaks and moves creates the feeling of a simple man.

Although dominant while wrestling, Tatum exhibits a paradoxically sub-servient behavior in his everyday life, playing someone who is easily led and manipulated by others. He lives in the shadow of his brother and has few marketable skills other than wrestling. We see a man who is dependent on someone else and who is depressed about his inability to cope with his life.

Mark Ruffalo as David Schultz and Channing Tatum as his emotionally challenged brother, Mark Schultz, in Foxcatcher. (Sony Pictures.)

As Mark Schultz's coach, John du Pont, Steve Carell uses a different approach to transform himself: prosthetics. While prosthetics are a wonderful tool—when you look different from your normal self, you will naturally act differently, too—it is the physical and emotional life you create that makes a performance. Carell goes beyond the use of pros-thetics to physicalize his character in the most consistent and realistic way, fully embodying a man who is haunted by his mother's dominance and his desire to obtain her approval. Indeed, Carell's du Pont is so uncomfortable in himself, as himself, in every situation, it is almost painful to watch. Carell's transformation into this character is so cohesive and complete that it is difficult to see the actor at all. You almost cannot find Steve Carell.

Any actor who plays this role will not succeed in embodying this transformation unless he is aiming toward the light, the hope, and the farthest horizon. As John Merrick, Bradley Cooper brings a childlike vulnerability and sense of curiosity to his performance that makes his presence onstage always truthful and playful. This is most effective as we see him relate to characters visiting him; Cooper energetically conveys that he wants to discover and learn who they are and what they do while also reveling in the fact that he is being appreciated as a human being.

Cooper opens this production clad only in shorts, standing in a neutral position, as an able-bodied man. Also onstage is the character of the doctor with a picture of the real John Merrick behind him. The doctor describes Merrick's deformities. As he lists each one, Cooper transforms, physicalizing each deformity until at the end of the description, his body mirrors that of Merrick: twisted, gnarled, and misshapen. Film critic Rex Reed describes the transformation in his review for the *New York Observer*:

> "…you see the movie star, gym-buffed and camera-ready, clad only in a pair of shorts. Slowly, a curdling transformation takes place. The fingers gnarl, the mouth distorts into a silent cry of agony that looks like a facial expression in a George Grosz painting, the left leg subtly twists, shifting the weight to his right toes, and the body turns into a pretzel until nobody from Mr. Cooper's ever-growing fan base will recognize their idol…He creates more of an impact with mere body language than most film stars can project with the most elaborate horror-movie makeup…It is here and throughout that Bradley Cooper's talent for living in the moment comes to life, elevating *The Elephant Man* to unimagined heights of artistry…he makes the human being trapped behind the hideous face hugely real and three-dimensional…communicating more with his body and voice than most of his peers ever learn."

In the musical *The Last Ship*, director Joe Mantello and choreographer Steven Hoggett helped the actors playing the shipyard workers move in a way that authentically expressed their emotional anger and their frustration at losing their jobs. They were choreographed to move in a way that was full of energy and excitement without being stereotypical

Broadway musical choreography. Their percussive movement informed both the physical and emotional state of their lives. They moved and danced in a masculine, rustic, earthy way that never sacrificed the reality of the play. Although we could see how desperate they were, there was both hope and lightness in the direction of their bodies.

The usual, obvious approach to playing all these characters is to hunch over and pull down, exaggerating the infirmity or challenge. A case could be made that this would be appropriate for Hawking, Schultz, Merrick, and the shipbuilders. However, rather than do that, all these actors chose to elevate themselves—playing against the expected and creating characters that are powerful, interesting, and touching. For example, in the later stages of his illness, when his body is almost totally paralyzed, Redmayne, as Hawking, uses his eyes to communicate light, hope, and humor as he watches what is going on around him. Similarly, although brow-beaten and depressed through most of the story, Tatum brings buoyancy and elevation to the moments when he is in competition or being commended by his brother or du Pont. As John Merrick, even when he is most gnarled and deformed, Bradley Cooper is directing up. (Even the real Merrick had to lengthen himself to balance his enormous head on his body simply to survive.) And although the weight of their misfortune is crushing them, the excellent cast of *The Last Ship* elevated themselves to express their hope and dignity with skill and flexibility. Technically, they had to lengthen to use their bodies more efficiently while singing and dancing.

Standing unified, the ensemble of dock workers in Sting's musical The Last Ship *(2014).* (Courtesy of Joan Marcus.)

One of the best ways to create a feeling of elevation is to go back to the horizon exercise from Part I. When you are looking out at the horizon, you are directing your energy forward and up—into the future, into the possibility of hope. This gives you flexibility, lightness, and energy, without compromising the integrity of whatever affliction or physical limitation your character has. Figuratively and literally, leading with your head and allowing your body to follow will always create a visceral connection to the moment, both for yourself and for the audience.

A great example of this is Sir Ian McKellen's Richard III at the National Theatre in 1990 (and later in the film). He used this process of elevation to emphasize his power and agility rather than his deformity and disability. His movement was nimble and economical, demonstrating he was still a whole person. Other examples of actors playing characters with physical impediments who used buoyancy or elevation to create their characters include Dustin Hoffman as Ratso Rizzo in *Midnight Cowboy* (1969), Bo Eason in *Runt of the Litter* (2007), Juliette Binoche in *Words and Pictures* (2013), Marion Cotillard in *Two Days, One Night* (2014), Matt Bomer in *The Normal Heart* (2014), and Julianne Moore in *Still Alice* (2015).

At the end of *Theory of Everything*, Redmayne as Hawking says, "However bad life may seem, there is always something you can do, and succeed at. While there's life, there's hope." You must incorporate this way of thinking into telling the story of your character. The most fascinating stories are the ones about characters who overcome their limitations and rise up. Hawking himself said, "Look up at the stars and not down at your feet."

JEAN-LOUIS

Discussing these characters reminds me of the time I worked with Mary McDonnell to prepare her for her role in *Passion Fish* (1992). In the film, she played a soap opera actress with a severe drinking problem who, after an auto accident, is paralyzed from the waist down.

McDonnell was concerned that the habitual tension in her neck and shoulders would hamper her ability to express the character's violent tantrums and sense of deep loss. McDonnell tended to tense up her upper body; because in the role she would only be able to use her upper body to express herself, she would quite literally be handicapped as an actress. She also needed to find some way to make her lower body seem completely limp and paralyzed.

For two months, we worked intensely, using the principles of the Alexander Technique to free McDonnell of the excessive tension between her head and her spine and to integrate the breathing mechanism to bring more fluidity and awareness to her whole body. Complicating this process, McDonnell was shooting a role in another film, *Sneakers*, as we were working to prepare her for this one. So, I would meet with her on set, and whenever she was not shooting, we would work on the Alexander Technique or work with using a wheelchair.

Although McDonnell spent much of *Passion Fish* in a wheelchair, there was a scene where she had to drunkenly fall out and make her way back to it, dragging her useless limbs with her. Because of the previous work we had done with the Alexander Technique, she had better coordination in her shoulders, neck, and back to be able to play the scene in a convincing way, without hurting herself.

McDonnell did a masterful job of playing an imperious, mercurial soap opera actress, incorporating her alcoholism, her struggle with her disability, her tempestuous relationship with her caregiver, and her romantic relationship with her boyfriend (the brilliant David Strathairn) into her performance. She created a vivid, living, touching portrayal of a human being.

For her work in *Passion Fish*, McDonnell was honored with an Oscar nomination for Best Actress in 1992.

One of the most rewarding things about my job is getting to work with people over the years. They change, I change. More than 20 years later, I got to work with McDonnell again as she prepared to play Madame Ranevskaya in *The Cherry Orchard* at the People's Light Theatre—again opposite David Strathairn.

REVIEW: PART III

After reading Part III and attempting the explorations we have guided you through, you should now be comfortable, and capable of, doing the following:

- Approaching and reading the script through character
- Creating and using both a character biography and a character map
- Working with character archetypes
- Integrating music and rhythm into your discovery of character
- Enhancing and animating your character through imagery
- Building a fully realized character through animal studies
- Playing physical and emotional differences

If, upon reading this list, you realize there are any concepts you are not clear about, we recommend you go back and refresh your cognitive and emotional memory before you move on. The information and experiences you have gained throughout this book thus far will be most helpful to you if you work at retaining them and bringing each experience you've had with the material to every step of your living process as an actor.

PART IV

INTEGRATING COSTUMES, PROPS, AND SETS WITH YOUR VISION OF THE CHARACTER

Now that you have developed the internal, psychological, and emotional reality of your character, and you are able to color their movement, voice, background, hopes, and dreams through music, rhythm, imagery, and animal work, you are ready to discover and incorporate several external tools that will allow you to bring your character to life: the costumes you will wear, the props you will handle, and the sets and environment that you will live in. These will enable you to not just be a character in a story but to convey an authentic human being.

THE SECOND SKIN: COSTUMES

All truly great actors understand the importance of costumes as a tool for expressing character. In a 2006 interview published by MovieWeb, Meryl Streep admitted:

> "I'm a notorious pain in the butt for any costume designer because I have so many opinions. I feel very strongly that we make decisions about what we're giving to the world, what we're withholding from the world, by virtue of what we put on our bodies."

Not surprisingly, Meryl Streep's extraordinary range and flexibility are enhanced by her use of costumes in transforming herself. Although it is the same actress, notice how in all these photos, the costumes tell you so much about the character!

From left to right: Meryl Streep as Julia Child in Julie & Julia *(2009), Ethel Rosenberg in* Angels in America *(2003), and Karen Blixen in* Out of Africa *(1985). Streep has always understood the importance of costumes in informing character.* (Photos from Left to Right: Columbia Pictures, HBO, Universal Pictures.)

Although the director orchestrates the overarching vision of the story and characters, your vocal coaches, dialect coaches, and choreographers will help you move and speak in the world you inhabit; the set designer will create a vivid and functional space for you to move in; and your collaboration with the costume designer is perhaps the most crucial. Your clothes both inform and are informed by the period in which your character lives. The political conditions and social mores of the time dictate what you wear and how you move in it.

The clothing a character wears communicates who the character thinks they are in the world, their social standing, their psychological disposition, their emotional state, and how comfortable they are in their own skin. When you take residence in your costume, it affects how you move and function in your daily life—opening doors, sitting down, eating, addressing people, and so on.

Daniel Day-Lewis is a chameleon, playing different characters in various time periods and genres, which affects how he wears and moves in costumes. From left to right: Phantom Thread *(2017),* Lincoln *(2012), and* Gangs of New York *(2002).*

(Photos from Left to Right: Focus Features, Touchstone Pictures, Miramax.)

Costumes for period plays and films pose special challenges for actors. As you explore your behavior when wearing period costumes, you must comprehend the political, social, economic, religious, philosophical, artistic, musical, and architectural aspects of life during that period. Realistically embodying a character in a specific period of history requires a great deal of research.

> **NOTE:** Regardless of what period you are exploring, your character must be a living and breathing human being. If the audience cannot connect to and empathize with your character, you have failed to bring life to the role.

Looking at photos, paintings, and sculptures, and listening to music from your character's time period will enhance your understanding of that period and help you adjust your comportment and movement accordingly.

For example, during the 18th century, the S curve, popularized by English painter and engraver William Hogarth (1697–1764) acted as an aesthetic ideal and was integrated into every form of artistic activity. As 18th-century movement expert Alicia M. Annas observes in her essay, "The Elegant Art of Movement":

> "This asymmetrical serpentine line was proclaimed the perfect line of beauty. Its languid curve decorated every aspect of eighteenth-century life, from clothing to furniture to interior design, architecture, and landscaping, and also served as an integral part of movement. People walked, stood, and even gestured in 'S' curved patterns, a far cry from the dominant straight lines so popular today."

THE S CURVE

In the painting "The Bolt" by Jean-Honoré Fragonard (1732–1806), one can clearly see the S curve in the woman's body in ecstasy and the expansive movement of her male lover after the kiss. They are almost suspended in slow motion in their passion, but yet still performing the aesthetic movement preferred in this period.

"The Bolt" by Jean-Honoré Fragonard.

For the film *Barry Lyndon* (1975), set primarily in 18th-century England, Stanley Kubrick studied extensively the painters and the paintings of the day and extracted the shapes and movements he saw—including the *S* curve. In watching the scenes at court in *Barry Lyndon*, you can observe the application of Kubrick's understanding of this movement. There is a love scene on the moonlit terrace of the palace when Ryan O'Neal, as Lyndon, approaches Marisa Berenson to kiss her. Like the lovers in Fragonard's painting, O'Neal's approach appears to be almost in slow motion—suspended in space. His body is soft and curved, and the spines of both actors appear like trees bending in the wind. The whole scene looks like an 18th-century painting.

Ryan O'Neal and Marisa Berenson in Barry Lyndon. *It is apparent that Director Stanley Kubrick applied the S curve to the staging of this romantic scene.*

Another way to gain an understanding of the social mores, dress, and movement of a particular time is to watch period films. The following sidebar contains a list of iconic period films that take place at different times in history.

ICONIC PERIOD WORKS

- ***The Lion in Winter* (1968):** England in the Middle Ages

- ***Shakespeare in Love* (1998):** England in the late 16th century

- ***Sense and Sensibility* (1995):** England in the late 18th century

- ***Gangs of New York* (2002):** New York in 1863

- ***Unforgiven* (1992):** The American West in the late 19th century

- ***The Last Emperor* (1987):** Beijing in the early 20th century

- ***A Passage to India* (1984):** British India in the 1920s

- ***Chinatown* (1974):** Los Angeles in 1937

- ***12 Angry Men* (1957):** New York in the late 1950s

- ***Boogie Nights* (1997):** Southern California in the 1970s

- ***American Hustle* (2013):** New York in the 1980s

- ***2001: A Space Odyssey* (1968):** A futuristic outer space in 2001

- ***Blade Runner* (1982):** A futuristic Los Angeles in 2019

- ***The Crown* (2016) (TV series):** England in the 1950s

On the subject of movement, it's critical to identify variations in how people carried themselves in different periods of time and how their social status might affect their carriage. For example, Annas writes in "The Elegant Art of Movement" that in the 18th century, "Proper carriage or bodied posture was the cornerstone of eighteenth century movement; one had to learn to pose with studied ease." She continues: "Elegant carriage began with the head, which, as the seat of the intellect, was the focal point of the figure. If the head was held properly, all other movement followed naturally." When the relationship of the head to the spine was coordinated and moved with ease, the limbs were free at the joints—arms gently away from the torso without tightening, or in a straight line (usually a sign of a lower status or being a servant). The same principle applies today.

NOTE: The Alexander Technique is the most effective way to attain a poised and free relationship of the head to the spine, enabling every limb to move fluidly.

One of the most important forms of display and communication in period movement is walking. For example, people of high social status in 18th-century France spent a certain amount of time each day promenading in public, parading the latest fashions and indeed becoming works of art themselves. In this era, manners in speech, address, and etiquette in movement were the highest form of status.

The French film *Ridicule* (1996) depicts this practice. Even more, it illustrates the obsessive and destructive importance of *esprit* (wit), an ideal upheld by the highest level of society at Versailles and a model of intellectual life. Esprit reflects a cosmopolitan way of being, directly connected to the manner and cleverness of speech and social interaction. People could be completely destroyed and ruined socially by using the wrong speech, missing a beat in the verse, or addressing a topic unpopular at court.

Regardless of whether you are performing in a period or contemporary piece, you should wear your costume as frequently and for as long as possible before your performance. In most cases, you will not be able to wear the costume before dress rehearsals (or the day of the shoot), so you must find out what the costume is going to be so you can wear clothing in rehearsal with a similar cut, fit, or style. An actor wearing a long rehearsal skirt and high heels will learn to move differently than one rehearsing in jeans and sandals. Also find out if you will be wearing any specialized accessories, such as a hat, gloves, purse, cape, or a jacket or vest with several pockets, and so on. This enables you to create behavior and bits of business with your costume—for example, tightening or readjusting a scarf, necklace, or hat; flourishing a cape; and so on—to further inform character.

One of the ladybugs and Big Bill (a cat): Two costume renderings for a musical version of Archy and Mehitabel, *designed by Candice Cain. Learning about the cut, fabric, and look of the costumes as they began rehearsals enabled the actors to develop the behavior and physical life of their characters.*
(Costume Renderings Courtesy of Candice Cain.)

NOTE: In conjunction with your character map and character biography, costumes should always be used as a powerful tool for creating a living character, regardless of what period, environment, or genre you are in, or what kind of person or creature you are.

EXPLORATION: INFLUENCE OF PERIOD AND COSTUME

It is important to understand and experience the extreme difference between how we move, perform simple tasks, and behave today compared to how we would do these things if we lived in a different time. This exploration will assist you in noticing and experiencing the vast difference between the two. In this exploration, you will repeat the same scenario twice—first, as someone living today, and then, as someone living in a different historical period.

SETUP: PART I

The time is now. You are a person of wealth and power, and you are going to visit a friend at their house for tea and conversation.

You need to do this exploration with a scene partner. The focus is on your behavior as the guest coming to the house. (If you are doing it alone, pretend that there is another person there.)

You will need an empty space with a chair, a small table, and a few props: a teapot or pitcher, a cup and saucer, a dish of pastries or cookies, silverware, and a cloth napkin.

Be sure you are wearing hard-soled dress shoes. Do not wear any form of athletic shoes or sandals. Men should wear a button-down shirt and dress pants (no shorts or jeans). Women should wear a long dress or a rehearsal skirt and blouse.

Notice the casual demeanor of friends (Shailene Woodley, Reese Witherspoon, and Nicole Kidman) at a contemporary Monterey coffee shop in Big Little Lies.
(HBO.)

EXPLORATION: PART I

1. Enter your friend's home.

2. Walk to the table.

3. Greet your friend.

4. Sit in the chair and make yourself comfortable.

5. Pour a cup of tea.

6. Pick up the cup and drink.

7. Serve yourself a pastry from the plate of pastries on the table.

8. Take a bite of the pastry.

9. Begin the conversation with your friend.

10. Continue eating the pastries, drinking the tea, and conversing with your friend for a few minutes.

REFLECTION: PART I

- What did you notice about how you moved as you entered the room, walked to the table, and sat down? Did you move rapidly or did you take your time? Did you plop down into the chair?

- While you were sitting, were you slumping or were you energized and poised? Did you cross your legs?

- Did you adjust your clothing in any way before or after you sat?

- How did you pour your tea? How did you pick up the cup?

- How did you drink your tea? Did you take a big gulp? Did you sip? Did you savor it?

- How did you serve the pastry? Did you use your hands or a serving utensil?

- How did you eat your pastry? Did you cut it? Did you use both hands?

- How did you address your friend to begin the conversation? Did you ask about your friend first or did you start by talking about yourself?

SETUP: PART II

In this part of the exploration, you will repeat the actions you did in Part I, only this time you are an 18th-century aristocrat visiting a friend at Versailles. You have arrived in a carriage with footmen, and you are about to walk into an opulent palace.

As before, you will need an empty space with a chair, a small table, and a few props: a teapot or pitcher, a cup and saucer, a dish of pastries or cookies, silverware, and a cloth napkin.

Think for a moment about what you would be wearing for a scene such as this. If you are a woman, you would be wearing an elaborate dress with a corset and pannier (an undergarment that helps drape a dress in a more expanded way), and you would be wigged, made up, and powdered. If you are a man, you would be wearing a tight vest and jacket, breeches and white stockings tight enough to show off your well-developed calves, and high-heeled shoes with bows on top. The shape of the clothing and richness of the material would force you to slow down your movement and choreograph your every gesture.

"The Woman Taking Coffee" by Louis-Marin Bonnet (1774).
(Courtesy of JSM Historical/Alamy Stock Photo.)

THE ROLE OF PLEASURE IN 18TH-CENTURY FRANCE

Before attempting this, it might be helpful to know that in 18th-century France, pleasure was paramount. To return to our discussion of Annas in "The Elegant Art of Movement":

"One of the main goals of eighteenth century life was the pursuit of pleasure. Even the Declaration of Independence went so far as to proclaim 'the pursuit of happiness,' a form of pleasure, as one of man's inalienable rights. Note, however, that pursuit, not attainment, was the guarantee. This was a century oriented toward process, rather than goal, in which people believed that pleasure was important...worth taking trouble about, and could be given some of the quality of art."

NOTE: This exploration focuses on 18th-century France because the way people dressed and behaved then differs drastically from how we dress and behave today. However, you could do the same exploration, visiting a friend at their house for tea and conversation, in any place or period.

EXPLORATION: PART II

1. Enter your friend's apartment at Versailles.

2. Walk to the table.

3. Greet your friend.

4. Sit in the chair and make yourself comfortable.

5. Pour a cup of tea.

6. Pick up the cup and drink.

7. Serve yourself a pastry from the plate of pastries on the table.

8. Take a bite of the pastry.

9. Begin the conversation with your friend.

10. Continue eating the pastries, drinking the tea, and conversing with your friend for a few minutes.

REFLECTION: PART II

■ Did you notice differences between how you moved and behaved during this part of the exploration compared to when you did it the first time?

■ When you entered the room, did you look around and take stock of the whole room?

■ Did you walk to the table more slowly, either because of your high heels or because you wanted to display the finery of your outfit?

■ Did you find yourself extended and lengthened?

■ How did you greet your friend? Did you bow or curtsy?

■ As you prepared to sit, did you take the time to coordinate sitting on the chair?

■ Did you have a greater awareness of your body in order to move with the more complex and constrictive clothing?

■ Did you handle the teapot differently?

■ How did you pick up your cup? How did you add sugar?

■ Did you take more time to drink your tea?

■ What was the difference in how you served and ate your pastry? Did you take smaller bites?

■ How did you open the conversation? Did you inquire about your friend's health and ask about the latest news at the palace?

■ How were you sitting and what was your bearing?

EXPLORATION: TRYING ON AND PRACTICING WITH YOUR COSTUME

When you first try on your entire costume, you of course want to be certain that it fits you correctly and is not too tight or too loose. To ensure that you are able to use your costume effectively to embody and enhance the physical choices you have made in creating the character, you also need to be certain that you can move and behave as the character within the story while wearing your costume.

The Country Wife *at UCLA TFT with Adam Monscheim, Marcus Alexander Oberheide, Dash You, Lauren Dunagan, and Philicia Saunders. The cast of this production practiced extensively in their costumes.*
(Courtesy of Jennifer Bastian.)

The goal of this exploration is to not only make sure that your costume suits your character, but that it is comfortable and allows you to move naturally and easily, as if it is something you wear every day. If the costume design fits the character and the costume fits you, how you wear and move in your costume will create the reality that you wear this kind of clothing all the time.

NOTE: Of course, *comfort* is a relative term. There are some costumes you will never be truly comfortable in. We are more concerned that you are able to perform the actions required in the scene.

Once you have been fitted with your costume, you must learn how to move in it and make it your own, as if the costume were your own skin. You want to reach a level of comfort where you can wear the costume and not let it wear you. When you physically and emotionally connect with your character while wearing your costume, you will realize that the costume you wear is not just an extension of your character—it really is your second skin.

JEAN-LOUIS

During pre-production for the film, *The Affair of the Necklace* (2001), an opulent period drama set in 18th-century France, director Charles Shyer arranged for me to train Hilary Swank and the entire cast to practice period movement with their rehearsal costumes that were similar to what they would be wearing in the film. This was especially helpful for Swank, who had never acted in a period piece or moved and behaved as a countess in Versailles. In reflecting on this work, Swank later said, "Jean-Louis taught me that an aristocrat didn't just sit down in a chair. She floated down. And she floated up and down stairs. She certainly didn't climb them, for that implies effort."

I made a video for the director and the actors to use as a reference of all the period etiquette and movements in the script—a countess curtsying before the king, a maid curtsying before her mistress, a count bowing before a countess, drinking tea, and making an exit or entrance in different ways, according to status. This enabled the entire cast to be on the same page regarding the style and precision of movement. The actors prepared and rehearsed for about six weeks before shooting, providing them with a heightened and practical understanding of the social customs of the period.

Hilary Swank and Adrien Brody in The Affair of the Necklace. *Studying period etiquette allowed the actors to move with poise and elegance.*
(Courtesy of Entertainment Pictures/Alamy Stock Photo, 2001.)

SETUP

Regardless of whether this is for a theatre or film project, you should perform this exploration the first time you try on your costume. You will need your entire costume—not just the suit or dress but all the accessories that you will be wearing in the production, including hats, ties, gloves, jewelry, wigs, armor, and so on.

> **NOTE:** This might not always be possible, but the more of the complete costume and accessories you have, the more beneficial this exploration will be.

If possible, perform this exploration on set. Otherwise, find a space where you can move about and speak freely.

Choose three contrasting moments from the script, when you are speaking and doing some kind of physical business. The best choices would be moments that are emotionally and physically connected, indicative of the essence of your character, or that are physically demanding and active.

EXPLORATION

1. Wearing your full costume, tell yourself "I have time."

2. Start from a neutral position. Allow your neck to release, your head to go forward and up, and your body to lengthen and widen.

3. Slowly move into the shape of the character. Imagine where you are in the story of the play. What has just happened before this moment? Allow yourself to transform physically and emotionally into your character at that moment. Step into the world of the story and go through your chosen scene and movement.

4. When you are finished, notice if there were any restrictions. Did any part of the costume or accessories prevent or alter how you performed the same movements in rehearsal?

5. Repeat each moment several times. As you go through each moment, observe both how you can move easily and naturally in the costume, and how the costume can enhance or strengthen the moment. For example, if you are wearing a cape, consider using it to add a flourish as you turn. Or, if you're wearing a vest, pull and straighten it in disdain when you rise up out of your chair in anger.

   Also observe whether the costume hampers or constricts your movement at all. For example, as you turn your head, does the hat block your sightline? Can you remove your gloves smoothly when you arrive in the empress's private chambers?

6. Make any adjustments you need to so that you feel comfortable and free in the moment.

REFLECTION

- In performing your actions in full costume (especially any choreographed dance or combat sequences), did you notice any instances when the costume impaired or restricted your movement? If so, in repeating the movement, were you able to overcome the problem or find some way to adjust so you could move freely and fluidly?

  If you could not perform the action comfortably, speak with the director and the designer so that either the costume or the action can be altered.

- In performing your actions, did you observe a moment when the costume fed or supported the action, helping you feel that you really were the character, living in the time and place of the story?

PROSTHETICS, PADDING, AND MONSTER HANDS: CREATING CREATURES AND CHARACTERS WITH DIFFERENT BODY TYPES

Sometimes you will be asked to play a character that demands a completely different connection to the body than you have ever experienced. For example, you might be playing someone with a physical difference who wears a brace that distorts their body, or you might be playing someone of an advanced age whose bones may be stiffening or deteriorating. Alternatively, you might be wearing an animal, monster, or creature costume that reflects a character with a completely different body type.

Whether you find yourself wearing a fat suit, body brace, or facial prosthetics, you still must have the ability to move and behave in the costume as dictated by the story and the character. In *The Eyes of Tammy Faye*, Jessica Chastain not only uses prosthetics, but she also transcends them to create a complex and sensitive human being. As director Michael Showalter observed in a 2021 article published by the *Los Angeles Times*:

"Prosthetics can almost be seen as an obstacle to giving the performance—the actor has to almost fight through that layer to tell the story or give their performance. Costume and makeup helps the illusion that these characters are who we say they are, but it's nothing without the performance."

Aliens, witches, goblins, and monsters require that the creature costumes and specialized prosthetics you wear *enhance* your ability to play the character. Although motion capture, CGI, and prevision may affect your character's appearance and place within the environment, you must be able to move your body within a virtual environment with freedom, precision, and realism.

This can be challenging. Sometimes, the initial design of a creature costume fails to take into consideration how an actor will be able to move. In 2002, Jean-Louis was hired to work on the remake of H. G. Wells's *The Time Machine*. In this film, the protagonist journeys into a postapocalyptic future where humans (the Eloi) live aboveground and a predatory species of humans (the Morlocks) live below. Legendary special-effects supervisor and make-up artist Stan Winston (*Jurassic Park*, *Edward Scissorhands*, and so on) was in charge of designing and building the costumes for the Morlocks.

The costumes for the Morlocks in The Time Machine, *designed by Stan Winston, were sometimes challenging to wear and to move in, in a believable way.*
(Paramount.)

Jean-Louis was initially hired to coach actress Samantha Mumba, for her role as Mara, a human. But early in the shoot, the producers asked him to work on the movement of the Morlocks as well. They felt that the Morlocks looked and moved like big rabbits and were not aggressive or threatening enough.

There were several challenges. Because their costumes were made of rubber, the actors inside the costumes became so hot that from time to time, they had to be cooled down with portable air conditioning. In addition, the weight of the costumes brought the actors' posture too far forward.

Jean-Louis developed a more aggressive and powerful stance for the Morlocks, including a way of moving and running that was more menacing and aligned with the characters' temperament. However, the weight of the hands was still a problem. Each one weighed 35 pounds and dangled limp and immobile from the actors' arms. Jean-Louis convinced the producers that if they wanted the Morlocks to move like predators, they had to rebuild the hands, mid-shoot, using lighter material so they would be more pliable and capable of greater movement. Once the new hands were ready, he rehearsed the actors and stuntmen in the Morlock suits for days, much to their chagrin. But when he was finished working with them, the Morlocks were terrifying—and they definitely did not look like rabbits!

In the 18 years since the release of *The Time Machine*, there have been incredible technological advances—not only in CGI and motion capture, but also in the crafting of costumes and makeup design. (Witness the incredible, actor-friendly prosthetics created by Academy Award winner Kazuhiro Tsuji for Gary Oldman's Winston Churchill in *Darkest Hour*, released in 2017.)

WATCH THIS MOVIE: *THE SHAPE OF WATER* (2017)

Perhaps the most astonishing example of these technological advances was the result of a collaboration between director Guillermo del Toro, creature designer Mike Hill, co-creature designer Shane Mahan, and visual effects supervisor Dennis Berardi, in creating the costume for Amphibian Man in *The Shape of Water* (2017). Inspired by *The Creature From the Black Lagoon* (1954), del Toro wanted to make a *Beauty and the Beast*–type story in which the monster was not only the main character, but the emotional center of the movie. According to a 2017 article published in *Wired,* he insisted that the creature have a "soul beneath his scales."

Starting with a series of sketches by Del Toro, the process of designing the costume for Amphibian Man involved creating three dimensional maquettes, editing, tweaking and embellishing the design, and using a life cast of actor Doug Jones, who portrayed Amphibian Man, to make a form-fitting latex suit.

A full-body rubber suit is not only hard to wear and move in, but challenging to convey emotion through. "For three hours a day," writes Roberto Ito for the *New York Times,* "Mr. Jones sat while Mr. Hill and three other artists put the thing on: the foam latex suit and gloves, the fiberglass helmet with eyes he couldn't see out of, the sharp fangs, the remote-control gizmos in his spine." Ito continues: "The suit itself was so form-fitting that Mr. Jones had to use K-Y Jelly to squeeze inside; when wet, which it nearly always was, it soaked up pounds of water like a sponge."

Despite these restrictions, Jones was able to express his animal life, behavior, and emotional existence. Indeed, although the director had the vision and the design team created the suit, it was the heart, specificity, and power of actor Doug Jones who gave it such life and expression. This was particularly impressive considering that Jones could not speak or even use his eyes to express himself; his only tools to communicate were his emotional, physical, and spiritual energy.

In our first encounter with Amphibian Man, he is trying to protect himself from his captors, so he behaves as a violent, destructive, predatory monster. We see his other side later, in the scene where Sally Hawkins, as Elisa, reaches out to him with the simplest act of kindness: sharing her lunch with him. In this scene, Elisa sets up her "picnic," plays music on the record player, places an egg on the edge of his tank, and waits for the creature to come to her. Initially, we only see Amphibian Man's hand taking the egg before he submerges again, but the music captures his interest. Eventually, he rises up, leans on the edge of the tank, looks at the record player, and then looks at Elisa to try to understand what is happening. Elisa signs to him "music," and he signs it back to her. In this way, the connection between them is made; the rest of the scene simply consists of them enjoying each other's company, eating, and listening to music.

Doug Jones and Sally Hawkins in The Shape of Water.
This pivotal scene establishes their relationship. (Searchlight Pictures.)

In the following montage, which shows subsequent "picnics" with the creature, Jones rises halfway out of the water to get more eggs. In doing so, he does exactly what we've been telling you to do all along: He leads with his head, allowing his body to follow, lengthening and widening in space. Although we only see him from the waist up, we see great power, presence, and grace in his stillness.

As his co-star, Sally Hawkins, observed in a 2018 article published by *Hollywood Reporter,* "This film wouldn't exist or work in any way without Doug Jones, and Doug Jones being able to do what he does. Somebody mentioned they thought it was CGI. How can it possibly work if it was CGI? You see his heart and you feel his passion and you can see his thoughts, almost. He is in a rubber suit, so it translates and it comes through. It is only magic because of Doug. It can only exist with chemistry. You are only as good as you are a reflection of what you are looking at."

In exploring the gestation of creating this suit from design to conception, we can fully grasp what a feat it was for the actor to play a creature who was not only terrifying but sexy. (Oddly enough, Jean-Louis had worked with Jones 18 years earlier, when he played a Morlock spy in *The Time Machine*.)

JEAN-LOUIS

Writer/comedian Julia Sweeney studied the Alexander Technique with me in the 1990s, when she was a member of the Groundlings and working as an administrative assistant. She wanted to change her poor habits of posture and behavior, which she thought limited her in her performance work and her life. Also, she did not want her own habits to be the same as those of her characters.

One day, she came into my studio and told me she had a colleague at work who she was confused about. She wasn't sure if this person was a man or a woman. She wanted to develop a character based on this person, whom she called Pat, and asked for help in developing the character's physicality.

Pat was overweight. The character slumped and moved like a bowl of JELL-O, often making strange sounds. We worked for months, first developing a balanced state through the Alexander Technique—training Sweeney to have a lighter head-neck-back relationship—and from there slowly transforming into the collapsed posture and fastidious movements characterized by the placement of her hands on her upper stomach. In finding the buoyancy in the spine, she was able to play the intense physicality of the character without putting pressure on her breathing mechanism.

Ultimately, Sweeney became a cast member on *Saturday Night Live*, and Pat became an iconic character on the show. The work we did allowed her to not only transform easily into the character, but to sustain her energy and physical health. Several years later, Sweeney wrote a film for her character titled *It's Pat*. She asked me for assistance with Pat's fat suit, which was difficult to move in and also became very hot.

The Alexander Technique proved useful in negotiating these obstacles and dealing with the long days of shooting.

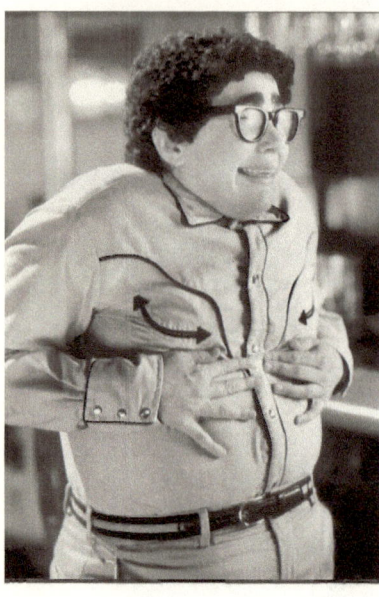

Julia Sweeney as a gender-fluid character, Pat, in It's Pat: The Movie.
*A summer shoot in a heavily padded costume made her so hot that
an air-conditioning device was added to the costume!*
(Buena Vista Pictures.)

Even though we have focused on period and creature costumes, every costume can be useful in creating a character. Sometimes, even accessories can help the actor realize qualities that otherwise would be difficult to discover. For example, a cape can give a character a sense of power and dominance, and a feathered hat can offer a sense of extravagance and status.

In the film *Coco before Chanel* (2009), Audrey Tautou's costumes were essential in revealing the inner world of Coco Chanel. The stark simplicity and the tragedy of her childhood were clearly expressed in her choice of what she wore. For example, her dressing up like a man was a direct response to her father's abandonment and abuse, while the dark colors she wore revealed her own view of the world—a sad landscape of loneliness and longing. Similarly, although it was the bizarre makeup that told us what a broken character Joker was in *The Dark Knight* (2008), the jacket that was designed specifically for actor Heath Ledger fed his unpredictable, reptilian physicality.

Audrey Tatou as Coco Chanel wears a bowler hat with a jacket and shirt that seem very masculine and stark in Coco Before Chanel.
(Sony Pictures.)

Heath Ledger as the Joker in The Dark Knight *(2008). The jacket, which was designed specifically for him, fed his unpredictable, reptilian physicality.*

SCOTT

In certain situations, when you are acting as part of an ensemble or a chorus, minor adjustments in costume and makeup design can give you an advantage in creating a more specific character. I kept this in mind when directing a Steampunk/Kabuki production of Gilbert & Sullivan's *The Mikado*. Because I have always been loath to settle for generic ensembles in the plays I direct, we dressed the "gentlemen of Japan" in this production in kimonos blended with retro-futuristic accessories. In collaboration with both the actors and the costume designer, I gave each actor an occupational or character archetype. So, although the general feel of the piece was feudal Japan, each character represented a specific type—for example, a soldier, lounge singer, governess, cowgirl, librarian, and so on. This enabled the actors to create interesting characters, coloring their movement and behavior.

Three of the "gentleman of Japan" from The Mikado *at Crossroads School for Arts and Sciences.* (Courtesy of Crossroads School.)

Though everyone was playing a "gentleman from Japan," each actor in this production of The Mikado *chose an occupational or cultural archetype, so that the ensemble was not homogenous or generic.*
(Courtesy of Crossroads School.)

WORKING WITH PROPS AND SETS

"Almost nothing in our character's life is what it is—but we must make it so! We endow the given circumstances, our own character, our relationship to others in the play, the place, each object we deal with, including the clothes we wear. All must be endowed with the physical, psychological or emotional properties which we want in order to send us richly into action from moment to moment."

–Uta Hagen, author of *Respect for Acting*

Just as you need time to adapt to your costume, you must spend time on the set and within the physical world of the play or movie to step into the story, period, and texture where the production takes place. Even if you have little input in the design choices of props and sets, you must identify how your physical setting affects your character's movement and behavior.

> **NOTE:** Familiarizing yourself with the set and creating a history of, and a connection to, the physical environment is an important part of preparation.

The same can be said for props. Any object that belongs to your character should have a specific meaning, history, and function. For every personal prop, you must figure out where you got it, who gave it to you, and what its emotional value is. That way, even those props you handle for only a short time can help you deliver a richer and more honest performance.

Your physical connection to props can extend, clarify, and inform the physical life and reality of your character. A colleague of Scott's, Virginia Russell, always ensures that the actors she works with are aware of the detail and history of every set, prop, and costume in a production. For example, before the first dress rehearsal for a production of Brian Friel's *Dancing at Lughnasa*, which takes place in a family's home in Ireland in 1936, Russell asked the set designer to add eight new objects to the fireplace mantel. When the actors arrived for the rehearsal, they noticed the objects immediately. Even though they would never handle the objects during the play, they spent more than three hours creating specific histories for each one. This ensured that every aspect of their environment fed the reality of the story and their individual characters.

During the production of *The Three Musketeers*, in which close to 30 different letters, notes, and missives were used throughout the play, Russell worked hours writing out each one in beautiful script, finding the right stationery, perfuming some, and applying seals with sealing wax and signet rings to others, so that each letter was a fully realized document that played a part in the story. It made a huge difference not just for the actors, but also for the audience, because it expressed the purpose of each document.

The props used as set dressing in Dancing at Lughnasa *at Crossroads School for Arts and Sciences provided an opportunity for cast members to create stories that would inform their characters.* (Courtesy of Virginia Russell.)

NOTE: We have all seen plays in which someone reads from a book whose pages are blank or a letter with scribbling that is unrelated to the play. Making each document appear authentic is a powerful way to convey the reality of a scene.

A prop can be an extension of who a character is and reflect their power—for example, a gavel for a judge, a scepter for a king, or a sword for a warrior. As Gandalf in *The Lord of the Rings: Fellowship of the Ring* (2001), Ian McKellen uses his staff not only as a walking stick, but also as a magical talisman that is an extension of his power. Indeed, there are certain characters in theatre and film that we cannot think of *without* associating them with a specific object: Aladdin and his lamp, Harry Potter and his wand, Charlie and his golden ticket, and Mary Poppins and her umbrella.

Four examples of the importance of props to personalize the characters. Clockwise from top left: Aladdin and his magic lamp in Aladdin (1992), *Harry and his magic wand in* Harry Potter & the Sorcerer's Stone (2001), *Charlie and his golden ticket in* Willy Wonka & the Chocolate Factory (1971), *and Mary Poppins and her talking parrot umbrella in* Mary Poppins Returns (2018).

Not every object you handle in a play will move you in the same way. (Sometimes a pencil is just a pencil.) But it is worth seeking out and considering which of the props that you handle in the course of performance you can find a higher level of connection with. Even if you do not have a deep emotional connection to every object you handle in a play, you still need to handle each one with specificity.

Most professional property masters will be aware of your character and its role in the story, and any prop they give you will have been selected to best serve both the play and your character. Sometimes you will be allowed some input into these selections. For example, if your character wears a watch, the prop master might offer you a selection of watches so you can choose the one that best supports your character choices.

NOTE: Once in a while, you will encounter brilliant designers who are willing to talk to you about their vision and how the costumes you wear, the chairs you sit in, and the props you use will affect the development of your character. But this is the exception, not the norm!

There might be times when you are assigned a prop you feel is not appropriate for your character. For example, suppose you are performing in Noel Coward's *Hay Fever* and the prop master assigns you a plain, wooden cigarette case. This would clearly not serve *any* of the characters living in the story! In such cases, don't hesitate to say, "I think my character would have a more expensive case." Although everyone working on the play is working toward the same goal, you know better than anyone what will best serve your character.

NOTE: Most directors will share the production design with the cast early on and explain why and how the physical world is coming together the way it is. Sometimes this information might not be available at the outset, however; instead, you will learn about the design elements as the story unfolds through rehearsals and production.

EXPLORATION: CREATING EMOTIONAL AND PHYSICAL CONNECTION TO PROPS

In Part II, in the section "Relating to Objects," you explored relating to objects simply in terms of their physical realities—how heavy they were, how smooth they were, how it felt on your body, how your senses were stimulated by it, and so on. In this exploration, you will connect to a prop on an *emotional* level in the context of your character's story.

SETUP

If you are working on a character in a play or film in which you handle a specific prop, use that prop in this exploration. Otherwise, choose a scene and a character from a play or film in which there is a hand prop that is integral to the story and the character. In this example, we have chosen to explore Laura's relationship with one of her glass animals in Tennessee Williams's *The Glass Menagerie*. This is a perfect example of a specific prop having deep emotional power and connection to the character.

THE GLASS MENAGERIE

If you are not familiar with *The Glass Menagerie*, read it now. To summarize, Laura, age 23, lives in St. Louis with her domineering mother and conflicted brother. An illness that has plagued her for her entire life, pleurosis, has left her frail and lonely. Laura finds solace in her collection of glass animals, which she calls her "glass menagerie."

In one scene, Laura's brother brings a handsome colleague from work (the Gentleman Caller) home for dinner. The evening's conversation is uncomfortable for Laura until she introduces him to her glass menagerie. In this scene, we learn that Laura's favorite glass animal is a unicorn.

Jane Wyman as Laura, delicately holding a glass unicorn as she studies the rays of light through it in the film version of The Glass Menagerie *(1950).*
(Walt Disney Company.)

NOTE: Other scene/prop possibilities include the glass slipper in *Cinderella*, the paintbrushes and cans of paint in *Red*, the quill in *Cyrano de Bergerac*, and glasses of alcohol in *Who's Afraid of Virginia Woolf?*

If possible, wear your costume on the actual set with the actual prop. If this is not possible, find a rehearsal space with some rehearsal furniture (a chair, a table, and so on) and, of course, the prop. If you cannot use the actual prop from the scene, find something that very closely approximates the quality of the object.

EXPLORATION

1. Pick up the object. Feel it. Relate to it and use it.

2. Answer the following questions to develop the history and meaning of the object:

   - What were the circumstances by which you came by this object? Did you buy it? Did you find it? Was it given to you?

   - Why is this object special to you?

   - Do you have memories of another time, place, or person from whom you got the object?

   - What is it about the object that makes you feel something? How does it make you feel?

   - Is the object handcrafted?

   - What is the object's history?

   - Where do you keep this object?

   - Do you carry the object with you?

   - What condition is the object in?

   - Is there a special way you take care of and maintain the object?

3. Place the object on the table and bring yourself back to the moment when you first encountered it. Was it something you had to have? How urgent was it that you acquire it? How much joy does it elicit in you?

4. Bring yourself to the moment in the story when you first handle this object. For example, if you are playing Laura in *The Glass Menagerie*, improvise the first time you saw this glass unicorn and answer the following questions:

   • Where did you see the glass unicorn? Was it in a shop window?

   • As soon as you saw it, did you know that you needed to have it?

   • What was it about the unicorn that made it special to you?

5. Improvise a scene in which you clean a special object. For example, if you are playing Laura, improvise a scene in which you are at home alone. Take out the menagerie, pick up each animal, and clean them with a cloth one by one, talking to each one as if it were real.

REFLECTION

■ As you were handling the object, did your personal connection and history with it influence how you handled and related to it? If you used our *Glass Menagerie* scenario, as you were cleaning the object, did you have a different relationship with each animal? How was it different handling the unicorn? Did you pick it up differently from the others and spend more time with it than you did with the others?

■ Do you now feel you have a different relationship with and connection to this prop?

■ Has this exploration affected how you handle and treat the prop?

■ How does the prop inform your physical life in the scene?

■ How does the object affect your level of energy and your emotional life?

REVIEW: PART IV

After reading Part IV and attempting the explorations we have guided you through, you should now be comfortable and capable of doing the following:

- Altering your physicality, behavior, and manner based on the time period and setting of the story you are living in

- Becoming comfortable and moving with ease while rehearsing in costume

- Developing strategies to handle the challenges of wearing prosthetics/creature costumes, make-up/fat suits, and other body altering enhancements

- Creating an emotional and physical connection to the props you handle and the settings you inhabit

Upon reading this list, if there are any concepts you are not clear about, we recommend you go back and refresh your cognitive and emotional memory before you move on.

CONCLUSION

BACK TO THE BODY APPLIED: THE POWER OF THE DOG

There's a reason Jane Campion won the Oscar for Best Director for her 2021 film, *The Power of the Dog*, the gothic Western starring Benedict Cumberbatch, Jesse Plemons, Kirsten Dunst, and Kodi Smit-McPhee. In it, Campion "once again [demonstrates] her own strong clear vision—not to mention superb control of her craft" and "proves her ability to illuminate hidden truths and let us see what was hiding in plain sight all along," says Ann Hornaday at *The Washington Post*.

Another article, written by Jordan Kisner and published in *The New York Times*, discusses the film's rehearsal phase, during which Campion "gathered the actors for a few weeks to hike, improvise, and do exercises," writes Kisner. The actors "ate together, cooked together or just sat in rooms, in character, not talking." Campion also had the actors write letters in character, as well as in other characters. And "she asked Cumberbatch and Jesse Plemons, who play brothers, to waltz together, to help them learn intimately how the other's body smelled, felt and moved, visceral qualities that boys who've grown up together would know," Kisner reports.

Benedict Cumberbatch and Kodi Smit-McPhee make full use of their bodies in The Power of the Dog. (Netflix.)

We were struck by how much of what she said resembled the concepts and practices discussed throughout this book. Upon further study, we realized that *The Power of the Dog* fully demonstrates many of the principles and skills that we feel are so important in training and practice. So much so, in fact, that we can use the film to summarize some of the main points of this book:

- **AWARENESS:** In the opening shots of the film, we get a sense of the expansiveness and desolation of the environment, and the isolation and loneliness of the characters who live there. All this is expressed without dialogue.

- **INHIBITION:** Throughout the film, there is a sense of quiet and stillness within the characters and how they relate or don't relate to each other. We rarely see them react without inhibition.

- **MUTUAL GAZE:** So much information and emotion between the characters is communicated solely through mutual gaze—how they regard or relate to each other in silence, often just being in a room or space (indoors or outdoors) together.

- **PRIMARY CONTROL:** Benedict Cumberbatch as Phil, the patriarchal figure, wearing his large cowboy hat like a crown, is in control of all those under him. His power is visible and apparent whether he is sitting, standing, walking, or riding a horse. When he moves, his head always leads, and his body follows.

- **GAZING AT THE HORIZON:** Throughout the film, the characters are almost always gazing at the horizon. The environment is both a setting and a point of view. Phil repeatedly asks, in reference to something on the horizon, "Do you see it?" During the brief courtship sequence between Rose (Kirsten Dunst) and George (Jessie Plemons), they take a break from their drive home for tea. They dance; then, holding each other tenderly, they gaze, with great hope for their future together, at the horizon.

- **PLAYING CHARACTERS WITH PHYSICAL AND EMOTIONAL DIFFERENCES:** All the characters in this story are emotionally damaged in some way. Although the setting is spacious and expansive, there is also a sense of alienation. Both the isolation and the self-imposed restrictive space they all inhabit together exacerbate their dysfunction, driving them to a breaking point.

- **WORKING WITH OBJECTS/CREATING RELATIONSHIP WITH PROPS AND SETS:** Phil regards and handles the saddle, bridle, and other totems that belonged to his late mentor, Bronco Henry, with an almost reverential wonder. Campion and Cumberbatch powerfully blend reality and dreams in the scenes in which Phil finds serenity while connecting to his memories in his hidden sacred space by the pond.

- **IMAGERY:** This is evident when we see Phil luxuriating and meditating with the scarf, as well as when he conducts his cleansing ritual after covering himself with mud. Indeed, this is reminiscent of the "Washing the Feet" exploration in Part II, "Wholeness: Expanding Awareness of the Self."

- **CHARACTER MAP:** We frequently see Peter (Kodi Smit-McPhee) studying anatomical and architectural drawings and perusing his scrapbook of fashion renderings, almost as if he was using them as a character map.

Speaking of Kodi Smit-McPhee, he spent time with Jean-Louis in preparing for his role of Peter. He found animal studies very helpful and used the fox as an inspiration in building his character. He also applied the Alexander Technique in creating Peter's subtle behaviors and in developing his gait, which contrasted with the way Phil and his gang of cowboys walked.

This book has taught you to explore the vast variety of tools that can be applied to live within a story, opening up endless possibilities to create honest, daring, heartfelt, and often unexpected portrayals of humanity in any period or genre. It is only when you explore and embrace all the possibilities of creative discovery that you can create magic and wonder and reality.

We hope we have inspired you to continue to work on yourself as an actor and as an artist—to expand your knowledge and the practice of your art and your craft. This is a constant, ongoing process. Your creative muscles are like any other muscles. Just as an athlete trains on a regular basis, your creative muscles have to be exercised, stretched, and kept in shape throughout your life and career. You must keep yourself in tune, whether you are working on an acting project, or not. The Alexander Technique can help you do just that.

alexander
techworks

CONTINUING YOUR EDUCATION IN THE ALEXANDER TECHNIQUE

This book serves as an introduction to the physical training of the actor and to the study of the Alexander Technique as a fundamental tool to develop, inform, and serve your work as an actor. You can use the exercises and theories included in this book on any project you are working on, regardless of the venue or size of the role.

Further study of the Alexander Technique is highly recommended, whether privately, semi-privately, or in a group setting. Just as professional musicians must continue their lessons throughout their careers, actors must also continue their education.

We hope that getting a taste of this technique and its value as a tool in your work as an actor will encourage you to continue exploring the Alexander Technique, just as you would continue taking acting, dance, and movement classes.

If you are interested in further instruction or in-person coaching in the Alexander Technique in particular or in performance in general from Jean-Louis or Scott, please contact us:

Jean-Louis Rodrigue, Director
Kristof Konrad, Director
Alexander Techworks
https://alexandertechworks.com/back-to-the-body/
info@alexandertechworks.com

Scott Weintraub
scottweintraub10@gmail.com

Alternatively, you can find a certified teacher of the Alexander Technique through the American Society of the Alexander Technique (AmSAT) by visiting one of the following websites:

- **UNITED STATES:** https://www.amsatonline.org
- **UK AND EUROPE:** https://alexandertechnique.co.uk
- **AUSTRALIA:** https://www.austat.org.au

APPENDIX A

THE FUTURE IS HERE:
NEW TECHNOLOGIES

Virtual production. You've probably heard this term used to describe all manner of fantastical-sounding technical advancements in the filmmaking space. But it's actually a very specific, and very real technology that helps actors and members of the film crew in powerful ways.

Adam Valdez, a visual effects supervisor who worked on *The Lion King*, tells us, "The way I think of virtual production is simply that it's where physical production methods and the computer meet. There is a clear interest from filmmakers to be more hands-on with all of this. They see it as a dry-run for making their films, as a way to get their creative minds into their scenes, and I expect actors will start to be more involved."

It is important that you familiarize yourself with the process of acting in virtual environments and become comfortable using it for film acting in the future. As virtual production technology advances, actors must grow with it, learning different skills to bring truth and humanity to the work of creating a character. This new way of creating cinema calls for actors who are physically and mentally flexible and are able to express emotions and intentions through their bodies in a clear way.

We all know that in making a film you do many takes. Virtual production requires a heightened level of precision through repetition that is different from what you may have experienced before. Applying this new technology to the work is so complex and expensive that actors are not afforded the luxury of trial and error in making a scene or a moment work. In the past, anyone who has done multiple takes of a scene in film or television has had the freedom to make minor adjustments in movement or their delivery as they try to keep a scene fresh and alive. With these new technologies, this is no longer the case.

Because the world you're acting in is virtual, and often, what you are reacting to and the environment you are in is not really there, you have to create your own specific reality in your mind and body. Much of what you have already done through the training outlined in this book will give you the tools and the kinesthetic awareness to fulfill the demands of this new way of working.

If you are connected to your body, your breathing, and the reality you create, it won't matter what new virtual tools are invented and imposed on you in the future. You will be able to work in any new medium. As you are practicing the basic principles of the Alexander Technique—awareness, inhibition, primary control, and direction—they will help you with the ever-changing requirements of this new way of shooting films.

Just as it is important to view a bulky, cumbersome, or constraining costume as a tool rather than an obstacle, you must embrace the sensors, harnesses, headgear, and 3D cameras that you will need to wear as part of your character when working with these new tools.

NOTE: Applying the basic principles of the Alexander Technique enhances awareness of the whole body in stillness and in movement, regardless of what type of environment you are in. Many of the skills and concepts you have already learned in this book will assist you in creating human reality in virtual environments.

JEAN-LOUIS

For several years, I have co-taught "Acting for Virtual Environments" with Jeff Burke, Dean of Technology and Innovation, at the UCLA School of Theater, Film and Television. This course focuses on synthesizing actors' gestures, actions, and ultimately their characterizations to create scene work for virtual reality and motion capture. By using short scenes from film scripts, actors immerse themselves in a collaboration to explore character using Alexander and other acting techniques. The goal is to understand how changes in the size and intensity of movement and energy directly influence the life and authenticity of the character in a virtual environment.

Students at UCLA working in motion capture and pre-vis.
(Courtesy of Jeff Burke.)

ACTING IN VIRTUAL ENVIRONMENTS

The big question is, how does virtual production help actors tell the story? Well, historically, it hasn't. But more recently, advancements in virtual production technologies have given actors new tools to improve their performance in virtual environments.

One such advancement comes thanks to a new powerful virtual tool developed by director Jon Favreau in collaboration with Industrial Light & Magic (ILM) and Epic Games during the creation of the live-action TV series *Star Wars: The Mandalorian*. This tool enables actors to see otherworldly environments all around them during shooting using a series of massive LED screens, collectively known as *the Volume*.

It's easy to imagine the advantages for actors when they can actually *see* the planets, spaceships, and other spectacular things mentioned in the script! Compared to working against a green or blue screen (or a tennis ball on a stick), the Volume provides actors with a greatly enhanced sense of engagement with their surroundings. This, in turn, enables them to generate more natural and convincing performances, with more spontaneity and reactiveness.

Indeed, ILM's Richard Bluff, visual effects supervisor on *The Mandalorian*, tells *Backstage* that actors receive substantial benefits from working with the Volume. "Feedback from our actors has been overwhelmingly positive," says Bluff. "Despite everyone knowing they're walking onto a stage surrounded by LEDs, the illusion quickly allows them to forget the artifice of filmmaking, and they are immediately immersed in the world we have created for them."

APPLYING THE ALEXANDER TECHNIQUE IN VIRTUAL ENVIRONMENTS

Many of the tools and explorations you have encountered throughout this book in your study of the Alexander Technique can assist you when facing specific challenges associated with working in a virtual environment. For example:

> **NOTE:** Several of these points reflect the syllabus for the UCLA School of Theater, Film and Television course, "Acting for Virtual Environments."

■ **DEVELOPING AND CONVEYING SPATIAL AWARENESS WITHOUT A PHYSICAL SET OR LANDMARKS:** By gazing at the horizon (see "Exploration: Gazing at the Horizon" in Part II, "Wholeness: Expanding the Awareness of the Self"), you can integrate the whole body between the earth and the space that you're in. It can create the illusion that you are looking very far away, and can also suggest a particular location.

■ **CONVEYING YOUR CHARACTER IN RELATIONSHIP TO ELEMENTS (STORMS, EXPLOSIONS, OBJECTS, OTHER ACTORS, AND SO ON) THAT ARE NOT PHYSICALLY PRESENT:** Using character archetypes (see the section "Working with Archetypes" in Part III, "Approaching the Script Through Character"), animal studies (see the section "Keep Me Wild: The Animal Within" in Part III), and natural elements like weather, terrain, temperature, and so on (see the section "Being in Space" in Part II, "Wholeness: Expanding Awareness of the Self.") can help you develop a physical character. This in turn enables you to move and express in a space that exists only virtually. Your nervous system and kinesthetic awareness help you to sense the environment and the objects that you are touching. Actors must develop their sense memory and bring it alive within the scene, regardless of what is physically or virtually present.

■ **CONVEYING YOUR CHARACTER THROUGH THE SILHOUETTE IN WIDE/MEDIUM SHOTS:** Similar to shadow puppets, an articulated and free body can establish character and intention. Having access to freedom of movement is necessary while acting in wide and medium shots. The Alexander Technique can bring extraordinary ease and flexibility to the actor. An excellent example of this theory put into practice is James McAvoy's work as the faun Mr. Tumnus in *The Lion, the Witch and the Wardrobe*. His articulated gait and the way he carried his body as he trotted through the snow was clearly goat-like, especially in wide shots.

- **REDUCING THE IMPACT OF MENTAL AND PHYSICAL STRESS IN UNFAMILIAR/ABSTRACT ENVIRONMENTS:** Practicing the basic principles of the Alexander Technique (inhibition, awareness, primary control, and direction) will prepare you to move in technically complicated and restrictive environments. Virtual environments are often used in action and science fiction projects, and actors may be asked to perform physical movements and dangerous stunts. The Alexander Technique can help you find ease in the quality of your movement, preventing injury while maintaining performance.

One more thing: In virtual reality or motion capture, one aspect often overlooked by actors and animators in their portrayal of a role is the character's use of breath and how it affects the placement of the voice, the development of signature gestures, and physical character nuance.

> **TIP:** During technical rehearsals, it is most helpful for the director, the technical crew, and you, as the actor, to maintain consistency in your character's movement throughout the scene. Don't drop your energy or distract yourself with other activities; rather, stay in your body and in the world of the scene. This will serve your character and the story.

JEAN-LOUIS

Gavin Robins is an internationally acclaimed director of visual and physical theatre. His work combines daring physical performance with emerging technologies, including digital media, animation, animatronics, automation, and transformative scenic design.

In 2000, Gavin was a key performer and choreographer for the opening ceremony of the Sydney Olympics. In 2018, he opened *King Kong* on Broadway, serving as the movement and aerial director. Other credits include the DreamWorks arena spectacular *How to Train Your Dragon* (World Tour) and the *War Horse* stage show (Australian Tour). Gavin has directed movement at the Sydney Opera House, the Sydney Theatre Company, and the Bell Shakespeare Company, and for award-winning large-scale events in Europe and the Middle East. Gavin is the Head of Movement at the National Institute of Dramatic Arts in Australia.

Gavin and I had long been aware of each other's work. The chances that we would meet were slim, however, given that Gavin lives in Sydney, and I live in Los Angeles. What brought us together was a grant awarded to Gavin by the Winston Churchill Trust to explore and research different ways to approach the development of character through movement and physicality in the United States. He spent a month with me, immersing himself in an intensive study of the Alexander Technique, animal work, and my method of assisting actors in developing characters. Several years later, I was invited to work in Australia, and I reconnected with Gavin, where we had some conversations about his movement work and the future training of actors.

Regarding the skills needed by the actor/performer in a virtual environment, Gavin said, "I look at films like *Gravity* and I look at Sandra Bullock and the physical training she had to go through. She was having to learn how to support herself in an aerial system and not only deal with being choreographed in three-dimensional space, but she had to be aware of cameras robotically choreographed around her and also what was being projected on the lightbox behind her. What I'm interested in for the future is how actors are able to interact and be available in their physical skill sets to tell stories with the confluence of projection technology, automation technologies, computer-generated energies and imagery, without losing the essence of the emotion and always telling the most profound story."

Gavin Robins and the giant King Kong puppet.
(Global Creatures.)

Ann Darrow (Esther Hannaford), King Kong, and his puppeteers
(The King's Men) from the Melbourne production of King Kong.
(Jeff Busby.)

Ann Darrow (Christiani Pitts) and King Kong from the Broadway production of King Kong. (Courtesy of Joan Marcus.)

APPENDIX B

FULL AND PARTIAL WARMUPS

It is not always easy to make the transition from the frantic daily routine of our lives to our actor selves when preparing to perform, rehearse, or audition. The first step to doing vital and exciting work is to let go of the pressure and tension of our everyday lives to warm up our bodies and senses to serve the story and the character.

There are many different ways to warm up, and it is important to find what works for you. Depending on the situation, you might or might not have the time or space to do an extensive warmup. While some directors start their rehearsals with a company warmup, others will expect you to be warmed up and ready to work at the start of rehearsals.

Regardless, you need to find a way of warming up your instrument that you can do repeatedly as needed so it becomes seamless and familiar—integrated into your neuromuscular system and thus easily accessible. This will help you ensure that your instrument is energized and tuned up.

Although the length of the warmup process may vary, every effective warmup includes attention to your body, your breath, your voice, and your mind. Depending on the genre and style of the material you are working on, we have found that the most useful warmups not only prepare you physically and vocally, but also act as a bridge into the world and time of the story. The use of both imagery and animal work in your warmup provides you with a heightened level of connection to and awareness of the work you are about to engage in.

Watching actors in rehearsal, it is easy to notice which ones have put in the time and energy beforehand to prepare themselves and which haven't. The ones who have are present physically and emotionally, picking up right where they left off in the previous rehearsal and building on the specific work they have already done. The ones who have not use the rehearsal time to remember where they were and what they were doing—not so much in terms of where they were standing or what they were saying, but in integrating rhythm, imagery, animal work, or research they were using for their character and incorporating any notes they had been given.

An actor who is actively engaging in the work of creating a character and story will grow in the role through repetition of physical and emotional actions until they get to the point where they become integrated. In the same way, through repetition, your warmup will become seamless and second nature. Memory and awareness are not only functions of the brain, but of your entire psycho-physical being. Science has proven that even when we believe a specific memory has been lost, it remains in the nucleus of our cells. A more basic explanation of this phenomenon is muscle memory. When we do actions repeatedly and mindfully, they become part of us.

What follows are various warmup exercises that you can adapt to the needs and conditions of various situations—time, space restrictions, and so on. We encourage you to experiment and discover what works best for you.

COMPLETE WARMUP

This complete warmup, which includes seven components, is the most thorough and beneficial, as it gives attention to each facet of yourself and your body that you want to warm up. If you put in the time and energy to do this entire warmup, you will be totally prepared for whatever work you are about to do.

Each component of this complete warmup is taken from explorations you've already done (with the exception of the "All of Me," component at the end of this sequence), so you should be familiar with them. If you need more clarification or have not done any of these already, refer to the original explanation. The components are as follows:

- Constructive rest

- Breath coordination and the voice

- Gazing at the horizon

- Kinesphere

- Direction

- Head-ribcage-pelvis

- All of me

The full warmup typically takes about 30 to 40 minutes. If you don't have that much time, choose which exercises will be most beneficial in the context of whatever you are about to do. Sometimes all you need is one or two of these warmups to get yourself focused and connected to your body.

CONSTRUCTIVE REST

1. Lie down on the mat with a couple of paperback books under your head, right on the occipital bone, located at the bottom of the skull before it descends to the rest of the neck. The goal is to provide enough support for the head so that it is balanced at the top of the spine.

2. Bend your knees, with your feet flat on the ground, heels hip-width apart. Place your hands on your stomach, not touching each other, with your elbows bent and resting at your sides. This will help you release the tension in your shoulders and experience width in your back.

3. Gently pressing your feet down, peel your sacrum off the floor, raising your pelvis up toward the ceiling.

4. Once your pelvis is raised, place the palms of your hands underneath your buttocks. Then, breathing out, gently lower your pelvis vertebra by vertebra, using your hands to guide your pelvis away from your head as you lower it to the ground. As you allow your spine to lengthen on the mat, do not stiffen your neck. Your main objective is to allow something to happen, rather than pushing or forcing it to happen.

   Think of your breaths as waves of water moving through you. By breathing like this, you become more aware of the map of your whole body.

5. As you are lying in this position, allow gravity to release your torso even farther into the mat. Gravity and the floor will become your best friends as you observe yourself from the top of your head to your lower back. Include your arms and legs in this awareness.

6. Wherever you are in your breathing cycle, allow a sigh to flow out as you whisper "AHHHHH." Feel the vibration of the breath and sound moving through your whole body. Continue letting each breath come out on an "AH." Do not push to take large, deep inhalations of breath. As you focus on the exhalation of the whispered "AH," your body will automatically take in the breath you need.

   You might notice that some breaths are larger than others, just as some ocean waves are larger than others. These currents of breath will continue to massage your internal viscera (all the organs and soft tissues inside your body).

   You might also notice areas of tension and bundles of muscular contractions, or even whole areas of your body that seem absent. Do not try to shift, fix, or compensate for these areas. Instead, allow your breath to enter these centers of tension.

NOTE: This is not a time for fixing things. It is a time for taking stock, with the intent of noticing where the tension is and seeing if, with each exhalation and inhalation, breathing and gravity will help everything shift and settle organically. Remember, what you do not feel about yourself is as important as what you do feel.

7. After you spend 15-20 minutes lying down, notice that you have a clearer understanding of your body map. Although you might not have a picture of every nook and cranny, you likely have a better connection to your body. The goal is to develop a curiosity of the self and to be willing to live in the question rather than the answer. Every time you observe yourself, you are encouraging your senses to attune to your body. You are asking, "What do I feel? What's going on? Where am I in my body?"

8. To transition to a standing position, lengthen as you gently roll your head either to the left or right, allowing the whole body to follow, so you end up lying on your side. Pause and breathe, finding ease in that position.

9. Leading with your head, continue to roll until you are on your hands and knees. Release your head slightly forward and away from your spine, so your head is not retracted back and down.

CAUTION: If you have any knee or hip issues, do not attempt the next step.

10. Bring your head forward toward the floor so it is supported by the mat and sit back with your pelvis on your heels in child's pose (in yoga, balasana). Keep your arms at your sides to help release your shoulders. This is a very relaxing position that allows the weight of your head to be supported by the floor, as well as allowing your spine to lengthen as you breathe into your lower back.

11. Like a snake, starting with the sacral area, slowly uncurl your body one vertebra at a time. Release the neck and let your head hang, working your way up until you are on your knees with your head perched at the top of the spine. Gaze straight ahead to the farthest horizon.

12. Gently allow your head to lead your whole body up, putting your weight on one foot and then the other, and slowly bring yourself up to a standing position. Take a moment to notice the balance of your whole body weight on your feet, feeling the same awareness you felt when you were on the floor.

13. Leading with your head, allowing it to move away from the spine in an upward direction, slowly walk around the room, observing the map of yourself as you move.

BREATH COORDINATION AND THE VOICE

For the following breathing exercises, we want to remind you that breathing is a natural occurrence in humans that should never be forced. You do not need to tell yourself to breathe any more than you need to tell your heart to beat. It is part of the autonomic nervous system (ANS) that regulates your breath and your circulation system.

When you consciously take a deep breath and try to "tank up," you raise your shoulders, stiffen your ribcage, and throw your head back and down, which creates constriction and tension. This is called para-doxical breathing, for rather than letting your diaphragm descend and lungs expand, you are tightening and preventing yourself from receiv-ing any benefit you would gain from a natural breath.

In all of the following exercises, begin your breath at whatever point you are in your exhalation. Do not take a breath first. The next inhala-tion will happen automatically.

ALEXANDER'S SEQUENCE OF DIRECTIONS

- Allow your neck to be free...
- To allow your head to go forward and up...
- To allow your body to lengthen and widen...
- To allow your knees to go forward and away...
- To allow your feet to go into the ground...
- One after another, all together.

WHISPERED AHS

1. From a sitting or standing position, go through Alexander's sequence of directions. You'll continue this sequence throughout this exercise.

2. Visualize, three feet in front of you, a friend, family member, or pet—someone or something that brings you joy or lightens your spirits.

   > **NOTE:** It is important that you think of someone or something real, as this will animate and engage you with your whole being, so you're not just staring into space.

   As you go forward and up, the thought of seeing that person or thing will enliven and lift your soft palate and soften your face, creating space in the roof of your mouth and the back of your throat, effortlessly, through non-doing.

3. Direct the tip of the tongue to the top of the lower teeth. This prevents the tongue from getting in the way, shaping your mouth to form the open AH sound.

4. Let the weight of the jaw bring it forward and down. Do not tilt the head back.

5. Whisper "AHHHH...." The sound should be almost imperceptible. As you go forward and up, visualize the AH going forward and up.

   Whispering is not a way we usually speak, so Alexander asks us to create the sound AH in an unusual way. The vowel sound AH (as in father) lets the air through with the least obstruction. You are not pushing to make a forced sound or a stage whisper. As you exhale, allow the vowel sound AH to lightly ride on the current of your breath.

6. After your first AH, you do not have to take a breath. Just close your lips, and the air will naturally come rushing back in through your nostrils.

7. Do several repetitions of the whispered AH, visualizing the air coming back in and giving you buoyancy and the AHs flowing out of you with ease.

SILENT LA LA LA

1. From a sitting or standing position, go through Alexander's sequence of directions. You'll continue this sequence throughout this exercise.

2. Visualize, three feet in front of you, a friend, family member, or pet—someone or something that brings you joy or lightens your spirits.

3. As you allow your breath to be released, silently whisper "LA LA LA LA LA," creating the sound by fluttering your tongue up and down. Allow your jaw to stay released, without engaging it.

   As with the whispered AH sound, your LA LA LAs are voiced almost silently, and do not need to be heard by anyone but yourself.

4. When you run out of breath, let the air come back in and repeat your LAs. Do not push the exhale. Tension interferes with the outward release of the breath and blocks the air from arriving in the lungs.

WHISPERED F SOUND

1. From a sitting or standing position, go through Alexander's sequence of directions. You'll continue this sequence throughout this exercise.

2. Visualize, three feet in front of you, a friend, family member, or pet—someone or something that brings you joy or lightens your spirits.

3. Allow your top teeth to rest gently behind your bottom lip and release your breath on an F sound. Make sure the jaw is loose. Do not push, squeeze or tighten on the exhalation.

4. At the end of the exhalation allow the air to flow back into your lungs and release it on the F sound again. Notice how all the muscles coordinate to support the movement of the breath.

5. Do the process again. Think of this current that is created as the air leaves the body as a column of air that is drawing the spine upward and sustaining the energy behind the sound.

THE WHISPERED F TO A PHONATED AH

1. From a sitting or standing position, go through Alexander's sequence of directions. You'll continue this sequence throughout this exercise.

2. Visualize, three feet in front of you, a friend, family member, or pet—someone or something that brings you joy or lightens your spirits.

3. On an exhalation, open an easy F sound to a whispered AH. As the F opens to the AH, allow it to resonate. Unlike the previous explorations, this AH is audible.

4. Explore changing the pitch as the F expands to the AH. Because you are amplifying the sound, you may feel it vibrating in your head and through your chest.

5. Switch from an F sound to an M sound followed by a whispered AH. You may feel the sound vibrating more in your mask (the spaces behind the bones and cartilage in your face behind your cheekbones, your nose, and just beneath your eyes, where sound resonates) and in your lips. Never force the breath, as unwanted tension pulls us off balance.

6. As you repeat, direct the sound forward and up and out toward the horizon.

GAZING INTO THE HORIZON

1. Place your feet hip-width apart. Make sure your big toe, first toe, and second toe are pointing forward, and that your feet are parallel. (A turned-out posture tightens the hips and lower back, preventing the neck from being free.) Allow yourself to breathe fully.

2. Tell yourself, "I have time."

3. Picture yourself standing at your favorite beach, mountain, or desert, and look straight ahead. Imagine you are looking at the farthest horizon, where the sky would meet the land or sea.

4. Letting your gaze guide you, slowly turn 360 degrees, looking at the horizon all around you, at the exact point where the land or sea ends and the sky begins.

5. Extend your whole arm, lengthening from your shoulder to your fingers, toward the horizon. Notice that your head is much higher on your spine and your whole body feels taller.

6. Gently pivot your head slightly up and down to allow your neck muscles to release.

7. Leading up with your head, and keeping your eyes on the horizon, walk around in the space. Allow your steps to be deliberate. Continue to look at the horizon as you walk. Be curious and investigate the space. Walk as if you were discovering details in the environment— say, a shell, a tree branch, or a stone on the ground. Be aware of the many sensations in the environment—the smells and sounds, and maybe even the feel of a breeze or the heat of the sun on your skin.

8. If you are working in a group, relate to the people around you. Recognize them as they recognize you. Alternatively, relate to people in your imagination. Spot them approaching you from the horizon —an old friend, a deceased relative you never made peace with, or a jilted lover. Greet them, shake their hands, touch them. Continue to be aware of the horizon within the context of these interactions.

9. Walk toward the center of the space. Stop and look out toward the horizon. If you are performing this exercise with others, share this moment of being engaged with the space and each other in a common activity.

KINESPHERE

1. Place your feet parallel to each other, hip-width apart. Feel the weight of your body on your feet, distributed evenly between your heels and the balls of your feet.

2. Notice if you are tightening your ankles. If you are, loosen them by gently shifting your weight forward onto the balls of your feet and then back on your heels. Do this a few times until you find the center between the balls of your feet and your heels. Be sure to soften behind your knees.

3. Gaze out at the farthest horizon and gently pivot your head up and down on top of your first vertebra to ensure that your neck and head move freely.

4. Imagine you have a searchlight that emits light from the crown of your head. Turn it on so that the searchlight is shining 100 feet up into the air.

5. As you continue to shine the searchlight upward, imagine your feet are growing roots 100 feet into the ground. These roots don't anchor or tether you to the soil; rather, they serve as a foundation—a source of energy and support—as they penetrate deep into the earth. Notice how this feels.

6. Imagine you have the ability to release the roots growing up, enabling you to walk through space. Before each footstep, release the roots that have grown into the ground; then, as you complete each step, grow new ones through the foot. Continue to imagine the searchlight beaming from the top of your head and the roots growing deeper and deeper into the ground as you move.

7. Return to stillness or, if working in a group, return to the circle.

8. Allow your arms to hang gently by your sides and imagine that each of your fingers is a tiny flashlight.

9. Turn on every flashlight. Allow a beam of light to emit from each finger and shine onto the floor.

10. Allow your finger-lights to slowly lift your arms up in front of you, open them to either side, and raise them above your head.

11. Continue to imagine the searchlight beaming from the top of your head and the roots growing from the bottom of your feet, and let your finger-lights guide your arms to move freely. Shine your lights on all the surfaces of the space.

12. Move and expand through space, remaining aware of the farthest horizon. Notice how this feels.

13. Stop moving or return to the circle and allow your arms to come to rest at your sides.

14. Imagine that all of your skin and clothing is porous and translucent, like rice paper. Now imagine there is a light in the center of your body and turn it on. It is a golden, bright source of light, and its rays shine through the pores of your skin in every direction.

15. Feel the light coming out of the center of your body, forward, sideways, and backward, illuminating every wall of the space. This light is not just a glow inside you; it is a bright, all-encompassing light, emanating from the core of your being, expanding you in the space. Breathe through every pore and ray of light, allowing the breath to fuel your entire being, and sense your energy expanding into space.

16. While maintaining this awareness and all these visualizations—the searchlight from your head, the roots from your feet, the flashlights from your fingers, and the lantern at the center of your body shining outward—begin moving throughout the space once again.

> **TIP:** If you are in a group, become as aware of the others' lights as you are of your own. Also, keep making random and dynamic changes in direction so that everyone is moving in different directions.

17. When you feel you have explored the space to your satisfaction for some time, return to stillness or, if working in a group, to the circle.

DIRECTION

1. Stand as you normally would—as if you were waiting for a bus. What do you notice about how you are standing? Do not alter how you are standing; just observe and notice.

   - Are your head and neck jutting forward?

   - Is your weight on one leg or is it distributed evenly on both your feet?

   - Is one shoulder higher or lower than the other?

   - Are you collapsed on the top of your spine with your chest caved in?

   - Is your pelvis pushed forward?

   - Do you feel heavy?

   If the answer to any of these questions is yes, don't worry. This is how most of us stand when we are in stillness. Let's explore how we can use the Alexander Technique to find greater ease and balance in our posture at rest.

2. As you are standing, allow your neck to release, your head to go forward and up, your torso to lengthen and widen, and your knees to release forward and out toward your big toes, with your feet engaged and grounded.

   Notice that we use the word allow to link each step. This is an important part of the Alexander Technique because both the intent and physical aspect of each step release and connect to the whole person. The goal is to bring directional thought into a specific sequence of actions that integrate the body. You are allowing and facilitating a natural sequence of events that give you the most coordinated and free use of yourself.

3. Observe how your weight is distributed. You might want to experiment with this. For example, allow the front of your ankles to release. Explore bringing the weight forward on the balls of your feet and then slightly backward on your heels, finding the place where your weight is balanced and distributed evenly between them. Do not stiffen; move your head, looking left and right, shifting the balance of your body from your ankles up.

   > **NOTE:** You are not trying to lock onto the "right" stance; you simply want to feel the act of balancing and fluidity, the coordination of your whole body in the action of standing.

4. Now that you have used direction to feel comfortable standing, walk around the room. Notice what happens and how you feel. Try to maintain the comfort and balance you had standing while you are moving.

   Most people, even though they have just found a lighter self while standing, revert to their habitual walk once they start moving. They may walk heavily and stiffly, their spine and head more collapsed, their hips forward and down. As they walk, they think of stepping down on each step, which encourages a shuffle or waddle.

5. Let's try this again. Stand still and repeat the steps you did before. Allow your neck to release, your head to go forward and up, your torso to lengthen and widen, and your knees to release forward and out toward your big toes, with your feet engaged and grounded. This time, as you begin to walk, continue repeating these directions. As you bend your knees, tell them to bend forward. As you go up, the foot goes down. The head leads up, the body follows— one after another, all together—just like a string of pearls.

HEAD-RIBCAGE-PELVIS

1. Stand on your feet, hip-width apart, with your weight evenly distributed on your heels and the balls of your feet. Make sure your feet are parallel to each other, with your big toe and first and second toes facing forward. Remind yourself that you have time.

2. Free your neck to allow your head to go forward and up. This enables your whole body to lengthen and widen and your knees to go forward. Continue this process of directing your body as you perform this exploration.

3. Place your hands on the side of your head, palms at the hinge of your jaws, and say, "This is my head."

4. Move your hands to the side of your lower ribcage and say, "This is my ribcage."

5. Put your hands on the side of your hips, palms on your ball-and-socket joint, and say, "This is my pelvis."

6. Repeat this process two more times, placing your hands on your head, then your ribcage, then your pelvis, while saying, "this is my head, this is my ribcage, this is my pelvis."

7. Move about the room and say "Head, ribcage, pelvis, head, ribcage, pelvis," speaking and moving more and more rapidly as you go. As you do, envision these parts of the body as one connected whole.

NOTE: As you perform this exercise, make sure that as you move faster, you bring your hands up to your head and do not pull your head down into your hands. Lengthen and widen your body as you connect to your head, ribcage, and pelvis.

8. Continue walking but stop doing the hand movements. As you are walking, notice what is different and how your body feels.

ALL OF ME

1. Stand on your feet, hip-width apart, with your weight evenly distributed on your heels and the balls of your feet. Make sure your feet are parallel to each other, with your big toe and first and second toes facing forward. Remind yourself that you have time.

2. Free your neck to allow your head to go forward and up. This enables your whole body to lengthen and widen and your knees to go forward. Continue this process of directing your body as you perform this exploration.

3. Allow your forehead to gently lead the head forward and down as you allow your spine to roll down toward the floor vertebra by vertebra. Keep your knees soft. This is not a stretch.

4. With your head hanging close to the floor, place your hands on your feet and slowly roll back up. As you do, say "All of me," and slide your hands up your body, as if you are painting it with the palms of your hands—from your feet, up your ankles, your shins, over your knees, thighs, pelvis, stomach, chest, neck, the side of your head, up past the crown of your head, until your hands and your energy extend up past your head. This should be one smooth, sustained movement, creating a fluid connection from your feet to the crown of your head.

5. Repeat this process several times, gradually increasing the speed each time.

QUICK PHYSICAL/VOCAL CHARACTER WARMUP

There will be times when you cannot take extensive time to warm up but you still need to connect to your body and voice so you can approach a scene effectively. That's where this warmup comes in. This warmup can be done alone or in a group. We have found it to be an effective way for the entire ensemble to connect with the material.

1. If in a group, stand in a circle.

2. Stand on your feet, hip-width apart, with your weight evenly distributed on your heels and the balls of your feet. Make sure your feet are parallel to each other, with your big toe and first and second toes facing forward. Remind yourself that you have time.

3. Free your neck to allow your head to go forward and up. This enables your whole body to lengthen and widen and your knees to go forward. Continue this process of directing your body as you perform this exploration.

4. Slowly shift and transform the shape, posture, and energy of your body into the shape, posture, and energy of your character.

5. Shift back to yourself.

6. Shift into a different pose that reflects the inner life and physicality of your character.

7. Shift back to yourself.

8. Notice the difference between your body as yourself and your body in the character.

9. If in a group, go around the circle, and have each actor say a line of their character's as they shift their body to reflect where their character is in the story at the moment they say that line. Then repeat this step, but this time, have each actor say a different line that reveals something different about the character.

10. If you are alone, go through the same process, but shift into five different moods or tones of your character, physically, vocally, and emotionally.

THERE'S NO TIME!

There will always be occasions when you literally have no time or space to warm up before an audition or a rehearsal—for example, you're late and you're stuck in traffic.

As much as we want you to be ready to work, we don't want you to have an accident en route. So, as long as you're also able to focus on your driving, you can always do vocal exercises, use Alexander's sequence of directions to lengthen and widen your body, and use the whispered AH to help focus and release, while still getting where you're going.

When you get out of your car and are walking from your parking space to the casting office or rehearsal hall, you will have a chance to prepare yourself and to focus and energize your mind and body. You can also use the Alexander sequence of directions and observe your manner as you move.

Remind yourself that you have a choice with regard to how you will present yourself as you walk in. There's nothing more attractive and appealing than seeing an actor walk into a rehearsal or audition breathing, present, and ready to work! If you arrive in a frantic state of stress and anxiety, it will not serve you well, and will adversely affect the quality of your work. Remember: You have time!

APPENDIX C

EXCERPTS FROM INTERVIEWS

FRANCESCA JAYNES

Francesca Jaynes. (Courtesy of Francesca Jaynes.)

Francesca Jaynes is a choreographer and movement director who has worked for more than three decades in film, television, and theatre in multiple genres, including costume drama (*The Duchess*, *Great Expectations*), family (*Dumbo*, *Muppets Most Wanted*, *Charlie and the Chocolate Factory*), science fiction (*Gravity*, *A.I. Artificial Intelligence*), fantasy (*Avengers: Age of Ultron*, *Clash of the Titans*), and music-based drama (*Sweeney Todd: The Demon Barber of Fleet Street*, *De-Lovely*, *Topsy-Turvy*). Francesca has worked with many of Hollywood's most prominent directors, including Joss Whedon, James Bobin, Robert Zemeckis, Mike Newell, Tim Burton, Steven Spielberg, and Mike Leigh. In Part II, "Wholeness: Expanding Awareness of the Self," in the section "Being in Space," Francesca Jaynes discusses her experiences working with Sandra Bullock in the film *Gravity*. Here are further excerpts from our interview with her.

Francesca Jaynes (far right) works with a dancer during rehearsals at Pinewood Studios. (BBC.)

GUYS AND DOLLS

We wanted to create a movement for the gang. I tried a little bit of animal work but I knew quite quickly that that wasn't quite right. It needed to be more comedic than that. So, we worked on exercises where they followed each other's walk, and where your ears become your shoulders, or you see from your kneecaps or you chat with your foot, or you find one particular part of your body that doesn't work. They developed something that was idiosyncratic for them—a bit quirky, a little bit odd. But it was quite funny.

Then we worked the same way as you work with animal movement, using percentages and how, they're under stress, then the quirk—that idiosyncratic movement—is exaggerated, that kind of thing. So, they felt it was from them. And because they were all slightly odd, they did look like a gang. Nothing had really been imposed on them; they just experimented with moving their body and messing their senses up.

A.I. ARTIFICIAL INTELLIGENCE

I worked with Jude Law for his role in *A. I. Artificial Intelligence* (2001). His robot character, Gigolo Joe, was based on Fred Astaire and Gene Kelly. The idea behind his character was that he could change based on who he met. So, if he met a Japanese girl, he would change into kabuki. Or if he met a Spanish person, he would become Spanish. We did a bunch of these. One time he transformed into a generic Hollywood musical character. We worked on all these different styles. We shot a lot of it, but Steven Spielberg, the director, thought the movie was too long to leave it all in.

Originally, I was only going to work with Law, but I ended up doing the movement for all the other robots, too. They each had a different job. There were road workers, an accountant, a nanny, a chef. So, I just looked at each job, and I based their quality of movement on the specific skill they would need for their job. I figured, if they were going to do that job for 24 hours a day, they would have been designed for utmost efficiency, so I built up a picture of each robot by concentrating on what job they did. Like the accountant. He sat at his desk all day, so I figured his legs might not be terribly well developed. And the nanny—she was very gentle. She would sing. I told her there should never be any sharp edges. Everything she did was very considered.

Spielberg needed the robots to be still most of the time, and then run. So that's what we worked on. With that knowledge in hand, you don't have to impose anything. If you tell an actor that the top of their body works but that their legs aren't terribly efficient, they'll give you a great run, because they're actors and they know how to do that.

Even though they were robots, I knew Spielberg did not want them to seem robotic. They were all highly advanced machines. So, I looked at animals. The brilliant thing about an animal is if it hears a sound, it focuses on it completely, and goes straight to it. But as people, unless we are responding to something that is really shocking, we take in a lot of information and often get distracted. For the robots, I thought we needed to get rid of all that. So, when I worked with the actors, we did a little bit of animal movement—more as a warmup, really, to get them concentrating. I got them each to create one specific move for their character, and then to build up until they had about 20.

TOPSY-TURVY

When Mike Leigh and I talked about *Topsy-Turvy* (1999), he told me I would need to learn about all the operas leading up to *The Mikado* by Gilbert & Sullivan, because the film itself was about the making of *The Mikado*. It was really important to him to go back to 1885; he didn't want any preconceived ideas about how Gilbert & Sullivan is staged today. But beyond that, he had a blank canvas, and he couldn't tell me any specifics at all. Figuring things out was part of my job.

One thing I did know was that I would be working with an actor-musician named Andy Serkis. I'd worked with him before, on a production of *The Threepenny Opera*. He played Macheath. I'd realized then that he was a genius, and I was so excited to be working with him again.

Serkis was playing John D'Auban, the choreographer. Leigh gave us a studio and said, "Prepare him. Do what you have to do to prepare him to be a choreographer." We discovered that the real-life D'Auban was from Ireland, so I taught Serkis some Irish dancing. We also knew D'Auban had taught ballet. Serkis knew nothing about ballet, so I gave him a ballet lesson every day, and we watched the Royal Ballet rehearse. We also studied the history of ballet. We took it all the way back to *commedia dell'arte*. We talked about Louis XIV bringing ballet to his court, and how that influenced the courts of Europe, like the court of Elizabeth I. And we did some galliards, which borrow certain steps from ballet.

Through our research, we found that D'Auban had performed in a musical act with his sister, and that he was a legomaniac. Legomania, also known as rubberlegging, was this dance craze in the Victorian era. One day, as I worked with Serkis on a galliard, I realized, it was the same as legomania! Suddenly, I understood that you can trace everything back. It was thrilling!

The thing about D'Auban was, he never stopped. He taught ballet in the morning, arranged mazurkas in the afternoon, rehearsed with his sister and performed every night. And he played the violin. Serkis is a musician, and he taught himself the violin so that he could accompany himself.

I remember Leigh saying, "If you can get Andy to the stage where he can choreograph without any help, that would be amazing." And I thought, well, I'm open to that, but is that really possible? So, we went on this journey, and at the end of the many months we spent together, Serkis choreographed me. He even sat down on the chair and gave me corrections. It was quite extraordinary.

My favorite scene in the movie is when the Japanese come to the theatre. I'd taught everyone a quadrant, so they'd know what dance to do in the ballroom, but beyond that, it was all improvised. On our way to the shoot, Serkis and I took a cab. Serkis asked me, "What other dances beside the quadrant were around then?" And I answered, "Well, the mazurka was a big thing." Anyway, if you watch this scene, you'll see that at one point Serkis—who manages to get into every single shot, and comes across like a comedic chicken—takes out his fob watch and says, "Is this going to take all day? I've got to arrange a mazurka at 4 o'clock." He got everything in, with no help from me, because of the work that had gone on before. It was just in him. He couldn't stop moving. He looked like a musical choreographer in 1885.

JACK BLACK

Jack Black. (Courtesy of Steven Perilloux.)

Versatile actor, and half of the greatest rock band in the world, Tenacious D, Jack Black first made an impression as Roger Davis in *Bob Roberts*. His breakthrough role in *High Fidelity* was followed by memorable performances in diverse roles and genres, such as *School of Rock*, *King Kong*, *The Holiday*, *Tropic Thunder*, *Kung Fu Panda*, and *Jumanji*. He continues to split his time between acting and music.

Jack studied with Scott at Crossroads School for Arts & Sciences for two years, beginning in 1985. Scott not only taught Jack, but directed and performed with him in several productions. They have remained friends and have reunited on various projects over the last 35 years. The following is an excerpt of an interview Scott conducted with Jack in 2021.

What is your earliest memory of acting or performing?

Well, early on, when I was a kid, I had a hunger for the attention and the love of the audience, even when it was just my mother and father in the living room. I have this memory of re-creating my birth, where I would put a blanket on my mom's lap and I would—this sounds really disturbing—I'd come out of the blanket, and I would be like, "AAU-UGH!" And they would play along and be like, "Oh, our baby's born! Yayyy!" And then I developed a little one-man show—I think I was like 6 years old—where I was born, and then I grew up and then I went to work and grew old, and then I died. And it was all this one-man show. And that's the initial spark that kicked it off.

I guess it's kind of always the same—always in some weird way pleasing my parents or making my parents happy. I would play records, and then I would go to the mirror in the living room—it's all about my living room as a child; that's where it all started—and I would sing the songs, or lip-sync these songs to the mirror, and also imagine thousands of people in the audience. I think this is a common thing. I think you could trace that back to all performers. All performers imagine thousands of people in an audience as they perform all by themselves in the living room.

It reminds me of my favorite Radiohead song, "Creep"—"I'm a creep, I'm a weirdo." It's all about wanting to feel *special*—the fear of just being one in a face of millions, in a crowd—you want to stand apart just to have an identity, to say I exist. I am alive. I was in this universe. You want to make that mark. I think that's a part of why we do what we do, right?

So, *The Caucasian Chalk Circle*. You called me on the morning of the show, of opening night, and you said to me—these are words a director never wants to hear—you said, "I can't do it."

I was bailing on you. I called you to say, "I'm not doing the show." Which is so crazy to think back on because I was serious. I wasn't joking.

We were doing a high-school production of Bertolt Brecht's *Caucasian Chalk Circle*. I think that must've been the only one ever to be done in the United States of America. Has any other high school ever done a production of *The Caucasian Chalk Circle*? It was so intellectually advanced and challenging, and I think you should get kudos for challenging the students at that time to tackle such a challenging literary piece. No one else would even consider that for high-school kids, and it was such a great experience for me. What a blessing to be able to explore deep, dark political themes as a teenager in school.

Anyway, as you can attest, I was a ham. I loved to get up on stage and perform. Nothing gave me greater joy than having the audience's attention. But alongside that, I had this paralyzing fear of being judged. What if people think I'm bad at acting? Or whatever. It's funny because I was playing a judge in that play. As Jack. And I was terrified of being judged by the audience, because there are so many great kids and faculty at Crossroads, I didn't want to blow it. And that, I think, is a huge part of the mountain for all performers to climb. It's that you have the hunger—you want to act, you love to act—but then it's also a terrifying prospect that you're going to have to get up in front of an audience and maybe be bad. So, you have to want it and love it even more than you're terrified.

On that day, when I called you, I was way more terrified. I was like, "Yes I love to act, but I don't want to do this." I didn't feel confident in myself. I had real terror demons, and I called you, and I said, "Hey Scott, I'm not going to do the show, I'm too scared, I'm sorry." And you said, "Can we just talk in person? OK, fine, you're not doing the show, but can we just get together and have lunch?" And I showed up, and we just sat at a booth and had a little bacon and eggs or whatever and talked about my fears and my terrors and about—I don't remember words, but I do remember that you basically said, "You know what, what if you do go up and just totally suck? Who cares? It's OK. That's what this is about. You're a young actor who is trying something out." Whatever you said, it made me feel like, "OK, fuck it, you're right. We've come so far. Why would I not try?"

It doesn't matter what happens. It's the experience. It's the journey. Go do it, and see what happens. That's why theatre is exciting. It's live, right there, you never know what's going to happen. And you did it, and it was brilliant.

You also convinced me that just what I had done in the rehearsal was already enough. It was there. The raw parts of the show were working. I should say, though, that you convinced me to do the show, and I went on to have an electrifying night. It was a transformative night, because I went in feeling such dread and terror, and came out so brimming with confidence. I was emboldened.

In *School of Rock*, you had this six-minute monologue, where you're setting up for the kids what their song is going to be. You're playing all the instruments and singing all the parts in one take. How did you do that? How does physicality inform your character?

I remember talking to Rick (Linklater) about it before, and I was like, "Are we really just going to shoot this with one shot? We're not going to get coverage and get different angles so you can edit later?" And he's like, "No, that's the beauty of this scene. It's just going to be one long shot that we're going to pull back and it's a little performance piece for you." I was a little nervous, but I was like, "I know how to do this. This is just theatre, you know?" And I did a few takes of it.

That scene is all about me sharing my music and my art with these kids. So, there's a little seed of truth in there about the fear and vulnerability of showing someone your work. If you ever share a poem with someone, it's always a little scary. So, I do the whole production, and I tell them what is going to happen with the instrumentation that's not there yet. I'm singing and performing, but also exploring and reading and telling them the stage directions of this performance that I have in mind.

I think a big part of it, too, is, I had written that song for that scene. There wasn't a song in the script. Linklater just wanted me to sing something, and I wrote that song, and it's got a kind of ridiculousness—kind of Tenacious D vibe to it, a "this is the Greatest Song in the World" kind of vibe. There was a gravitas to it, but kind of ridiculous coming from this substitute teacher. And the physicality of it. I didn't really think about that; it sort of came from the emotions of it, and I let the emotions guide my body. I'm this "teacher," but really I'm faking it, because I'm not really a teacher. I just have a passion and a love for rock.

But you know what I'm saying about the childishness—the magic, the magical nature of the childishness. It's like an essential ingredient in putting on a show. There's just something very powerful about freeing yourself up from the constraints of society and saying, no, we're going to put on a show, and it's going to be, you know, just like when I was a kid putting on a show for my parents in the living room.

That's the magical ingredient of that scene in *School of Rock*, is that I'm this adult who is in this position of authority, I'm a teacher, and I'm going to teach your kids how to play music. But really, I'm just this little kid who's having so much fun, and is trying to show them that they don't have to be all serious and "student-y" when it comes to rock. It's not about that. It's not about reading, writing, and arithmetic. It's about the passion and the glory of art.

So, the physicality of that scene really is just a celebration of music and letting the music move my body. It was a lot of dance, and I probably should tip the cap a little bit to Axl Rose. I think I did a little bit of his dancing. I definitely borrowed a lot of the physicality of that scene from the great rockers, and that presentational style of showmanship.

How does your work with Tenacious D inform your work as an actor?

I started off pretty hot out of the gate with that little cameo that I had in the movie Tim Robbins directed, *Bob Roberts*, in like 1991. And then I had a good long stretch, like 10 years or so, where I didn't really get any traction. I couldn't get any big roles. I would try to get some work. I'd get a little job here and there, and I'd go out and get my own apartment, and then I'd run out of money and I'd go crawling back to my mom and say, "Can I have my old room back?" I lived there all through the 90s, up and down.

Tenacious D was the first time that I really connected with material. And it was my material. That's why I think it really worked. It's like I wrote that stuff. I found my voice, and I took that energy from

Tenacious D, where I was doing whatever I wanted, because for all that long stretch of time where I was kind of struggling, it was all about just trying to give the director what they wanted and trying to anticipate what they wanted to see me do. Tenacious D was the first time I was like, fuck what anyone else wants me to do. I'm going to do whatever I want to do and not have that subservient fear. It was because of the rock and the performing live with this comedy theatrical rock band.

It was that kind of performance style that I brought to my work after that, in *School of Rock* and *High Fidelity* and the Tenacious D movie, that kind of opened me up. I was able to tap into a little rock-and-roll energy. And it's kind of infused all of my stuff since then. What is it exactly? I think there's kind of a danger and an excitement to a rock concert that's a little bit different than going to see a play or other kind of theatrical event, where there's almost a tiny bit of insanity. There's a little bit of crazy danger.

GAVIN ROBINS

Gavin Robins. (Courtesy of NIDA.)

As mentioned in Appendix A, "The Future Is Here: New Technologies," Gavin Robins is an internationally acclaimed director of visual and physical theatre. His work combines daring physical performance with emerging technologies, including digital media, animation, animatronics, automation, and transformative scenic design. Jean-Louis became aware of Gavin's work early on, and later had the opportunity to train him in the Alexander Technique. He reconnected with Gavin some time later, in Australia; there, they had several conversations about Gavin's work.

What are your interests in terms of research and in training actors and animators?

My work at both the Sydney Theatre Company, under the artistic direction of Cate Blanchett, and the National Institute of Dramatic Art [Australia's leading acting academy] with actors, singers, directors, choreographers, and animators is devoted to extending the craft of the visual performer. The considerable research I have undertaken abroad for my master's degree investigates the notion of what constitutes holistic training for the contemporary performer.

I have drawn on some principles of acting and physical performance that I think will empower and liberate the way animators will analyze, describe movement and ultimately create character, emotion, and storytelling. It is important to invest in the evolution of this aspect of our industry's work in order to keep all components of the equation alive and as vital. My aim for the training and ongoing consultation/coaching is to assist the animation team to find logical and revealing physical choices that will effectively articulate and convey the character, story and overarching vision of specific projects."

From whom have you drawn some of your most important knowledge, and what did those people teach you?

I think what's always very interesting for me is that gesture and character begin with the feet. [Russian avant-garde theatre director and producer] Vsevolod Meyerhold believed, as did [Japanese avant-garde theatre director] Tadashi Suzuki, that all of the gesture begins with the feet. And so, I have a big emphasis on grounding the actor, so that there is a sense that even when they're shaking hands that the gesture begins with the feet. And somehow that encourages the entire body to be involved in the character.

The other thing I work with is [French avant-garde theatre director] Ariane Mnouchkine's notion that the actor's most primary muscle is the imaginative muscle. Linking the imagination to the body is a real key for character. And understanding, just as a fine singer might know what they sound like when they're singing, an actor has to simultaneously understand what they look like and have an imagined projection of the character and of their body in space so that they can inhabit that character with a clarity of illustration. Meyerhold says that as actors we are, ultimately, illustrators. And if we don't know what we look like and what we're illustrating onstage, then I think that characterization can be lost. So, it's this really interesting balance of what's driving the body internally and what is the most profound sculptural form that the actor can create from the outside. It has to be told in a purely embodied way, where the imagination and the body are non-separate.

What is acting about, really?

What I find is that as an actor, part of the craft is about keen observation of humanity and human behavior. And when you look at [French stage actor and movement coach] Jacques Lecoq's work, he recognizes that as young children, we're imitating life. We play with imitation in order to prepare ourselves for life.

How do archetype characters inform your work?

The stock characters in *commedia dell'arte* have these recurring archetypes and common storylines. What's interesting for me is the archetypes set up a physical blueprint and a reference point for an actor. This notion that a child leads with the forehead, and that their head is oversized in relation to the rest of their body so it causes an arch of the back, and the hands to come forward and there's that sense of open wonder and everything's OK. There's an inquiry—this curiosity led by the forehead. This unlocks a really interesting physical trait and informs the gait, and is similar to the work that you do with animals. It can often open up a physical choice or a physicality that an actor may not consciously make.

Look at the notion of the virgin opening up the cheek. We look at all the iconography of the Virgin Mary, with this innocent cheek, this beautiful open quality with the cheek and the angles that it creates. It's a beautiful reference historically, and it's something that an audience can understand. When we look at the crone that leads with the elbows, protecting their body and saying, "Is that mine?" We look at the angular nature of it, and the closed energy when they lead with the elbows. That has a profound effect. When I'm opening with my palms, it's the archetype of the mother or healer. There's that sense of opening and welcoming, and that if we simply round the palms inward and lead with the elbows, there is an extraordinary transformation of the body. And so, I love the archetypes.

How have acrobatics influenced you?

I think that an actor should be able to walk on their hands as well as their feet. Because I was an acrobat and I could walk on my hands pretty well, not as well as on my feet mind you, but I was drawn to this because there was such a high expectation of actors and what they should be able to do physically.

ABOUT THE AUTHORS

JEAN-LOUIS RODRIGUE

Jean-Louis Rodrigue is an internationally recognized acting coach, movement director, and specialist in the application of the Alexander Technique to film, theatre, and television. In film, he coached actors and collaborated with directors in *Passion Fish, Vice, J. Edgar, Life of Pi, W., I, Tonya,* and many more. In theatre, he collaborated with director Larry Moss and former NFL player Bo Eason in his play *Runt of the Litter,* and playwright Pamela Gien in her Obie– and Drama Desk–award-winning one-person play, *The Syringa Tree,* both in New York and internationally. Jean-Louis has worked on- and off-Broadway, and at major performing arts institutions such as Berlin International Film Festival, Cirque du Soleil, Los Angeles Philharmonic Institute, Getty Villa, Geffen Playhouse, Royal National Theatre, Piccolo Teatro di Milano, Verbier Festival, and Royal Shakespeare Company. For the past 34 years, Jean-Louis has taught at the UCLA School of Theater, Film, and Television, and the UCLA Herb Alpert School of Music. Jean-Louis lives in Los Angeles with his husband, Kristof.

SCOTT WEINTRAUB

Scott Weintraub is an actor, director, and educator. Growing up first in New York and then in Santa Barbara, California, Scott knew at an early age that theatre was his passion. He studied with Bradford Dillman, then at the Pacific Conservatory of the Performing Arts, with Michael Winters, Donovan Marley, and William Frankfather. Returning to New York, Scott played Berger in the National tour of *Hair.* He then became artist-in-residence at Theatre by the Sea in Portsmouth, New Hampshire. Scott's TV credits include *Deadwood* and *Curb Your Enthusiasm.* For the past 37 years, Scott has taught and directed theatre at Crossroads School for Arts and Sciences in Santa Monica. Many of his students—including Jack Black, Maya Rudolph, Simon Helberg, Zoey and Emily Deschanel, Maude Apatow, Jason Ritter, and Maya Erskine—have gone on to have successful careers in theatre, television, and film.

Scott Weintraub and Jean- Louis Rodrigue.

(Photo: Todd Domenic Cribari.)

INDEX

A

F

P

www.ingramcontent.com/pod-product-compliance
Lightning Source LLC
Chambersburg PA
CBHW020438130626
46549CB00001B/202